# BUILDING A CONSCIOUS CAREER

*How to Build a Fulfilling
and Financially Rewarding Career*

Abosede George Ogan

# FOREWORD

I was a young staff in the communications department of Bank PHB (now Keystone Bank), then one of the fastest growing banks in the country (2005 to 2010), when I met Abosede George Ogan (then Abosede Alimi) the author of this book.

She was on 'The Intern, a very exciting business focused live reality TV show. The Intern, fashioned like 'The US Apprentice' show was a hit on TV. The show had 10 very young Nigerians, some fresh out of service year, being given different business task every week to solve. Each week, one of them had to be 'fired.' Bose was one of the young people on The Intern.

Working with Bank PHB, which sponsored the show, I had behind-the-scene access to these young intelligent Nigerians on The Intern. I was intrigued by their intellect and their ambitions. Even then, it was clear that Abosede was focused on what she wants to become after the TV reality show. She had a clear idea of the career she wanted to pursue and did not want to settle for less. She told me then that she would want to become the country's president and she did not say it as a joke. She meant it.

Years down the line, I have followed Abosede's career progression closely as she moved from one job to another and up the career ladder. Within a few years, Abosede has moved from being an 'Intern' into holding a key position in one of the most important organisations in Lagos state, the Lagos State Employment Trust Fund (LSETF).

In between she has worked with Bank PHB, First Bank, Samsung, and even started her own training organisation. The journey to where she is currently has not been a fluke. It has been based on deliberate planning and ambition to build a successful career and family life. In between building this successful career, she got married and had children.

What Abosede's life has shown is that it is possible to build a successful career. However, it requires deliberate planning which is what she is sharing in this book. If you have this book in your hands, you are reading an author who has had a successful career purely based on her merit and what she brings to the table in terms of value. In the book, she is quick to emphasize that the steps to building a successful career that she is writing about is based on her own experience, as well as the experiences of other people she knows and reinforced with years of research.

She emphasizes that she has had to study extensively to build a career that makes her proud. She also notes that 'career is a lifelong activity' and 'knowing that you will spend most of your life working makes it an important part of your life and you should aim to not only get it right, but also enjoy it.'

This is a significant statement because many people fail to plan their career and so end up failing in their career. Career progression should not be accidental and is rarely accidental, which is what the author emphasizes in this book. Those who have had a successful career have had to deliberately plan their progression to the top.

The author, in this book, talks about the importance 'passion' plays in having a fulfilling career. She writes that 'Building a conscious career that is fulfilling will require that you work on something that makes you happy.' As a financial journalist, and editor of the most influential and largest daily business paper in West Africa, I know this to be true.

The best journalists are those who love writing. Their motivation for writing is not the pay-cheque but by seeing their by-line attached to a story. They live to have their by-line attached to a story; that is where they get their satisfaction from. These journalists, who have a passion for writing, eventually become the leaders in the newsroom.

The author also gives a simple advice about finding your passion. 'You will know you have found your passion when you do work that makes you happy. You are excited by every chance to do that work.' If you cannot monetise your passion, author rightly notes, that you should find a job that pays you well enough to finance your passion.

One notable trend in the book is the real-life examples the author tends to draw from highly successful black women. This must be deliberate from the author in a bid to inspire readers to see what these successful black women did to become what they are today.

It would be a mistake to think that this book is only for young people just about starting their career life. No. This book is also ideal for those who already have a career. As the author rightly notes, there is no end to learning. There are valuable insights in the book about having a fulfilling career life and on what to do if you are having challenges in your career or even thinking of switching a career.

Readers will also gain a lot of insight on the authors view about volunteering and how it can be used to boost your career. Volunteering is a concept hardly understood in this part. Yet, considering the huge challenges we face as a country, it could be one of best platforms to make a positive impact on our immediate environment while at the same time acquiring new skills.

As a staff in Bank PHB, I was able to lead a group of volunteers to offer one hour of their time to teach at a public secondary school, which was not too far from the bank's head office. We focused on the final year students. Not only did the students make some of best grades in their final examinations that year, but most importantly,the staff that volunteered their time were able to once more let out their passion for teaching which their banking careers had buried. For many of them, the experience was very fulfilling.

I must say I strongly recommend this book to everyone just about starting a career and also to everyone having a career, whether great or not. This book will make you rethink your career, especially if you are pursuing an 'unconscious' career path. It is time to have a conscious career plan, not dictated by what it is thrown at you but one in which you are making a conscious set of career choices because you have a clear idea of where you are currently and where you want your career to take you to. The author has written a great book that will have an impact on your life because your career is actually your life.

Anthony Osae-Brown
Financial Journalist and Editor, BusinessDay, West Africa's most authoritative business newspaper
Lagos,
Nigeria.

# INTRODUCTION

A lot of people struggle to find work because they have not clearly defined their career path and/or identified how to get there and many who find work often end up disgruntled, burnt out, unfulfilled or financially dependent.

In this book, I am going to show you how to identify the right career path that harnesses your passion and expertise for impact but also ensures you get financial reward for it. The solutions I provide in my book will teach you how to take control of your career and oversee it to ensure you have fulfilment.

I started my career in 2004 as a Program Assistant with ActionAid International Nigeria. But if I am being honest, the foundation of what became a career in development started when I was in JSS 3 and had the option of going to an Arts or Science Senior Secondary School class and I chose the Arts. Though I was young, I knew the Sciences and the Commercial pathway was not for me, Aged 13 at the time, I was already part of a music group and we were popular in our local community.

So, while I am not able to tell you specifically how I knew at this age that the Arts was the option best suited for me, I am sure my reality at the time made it an easy guess. This was further confirmed when I went on to become one of the Schools Social prefects in my final year of Secondary School and the fact that the few A's I got in my final exam were in Government, History and Literature.

When it was time to apply for a University degree, it was very easy to choose Political Science/Public Administration as my preferred course of study. Bear in mind, that the most prestigious degree in the Arts at the time was a Law degree which my School had as an option.

So, here I am at 16yrs old going into the University to study Political Science/Public Administration. I am not sure what the trigger was but at that age I knew I wanted to do work that will 'change the world and make a difference'. This became my new mantra and I gravitated towards people, things and institutions that had this as their focus. The rest they say is history.

I always had people ask me about my career and seek career advice but it was not until I started working in my recent job where Iam part of a team responsible for creating jobs in Africa's largest city that I realised how critical it was for people to be conscious about their careers. Therefore, looking back at my journey complemented by research, I decided to write this book with the intention that I can show as many people as are willingto know how to build a fulfilling and financially rewarding career.

# ACKNOWLEDGEMENT

I will like to thank everyone who supported me on this journey to becoming an author for the first time. I appreciate you.

To my former bosses and the current one, my story will not be complete without you so, thank you. To present and former colleagues, thank you for featuring on my journey.

To everyone in my network whom I met along the way and too numerous to mention, thank you.

To the General, my Father and his wife, my mother. Thank you for giving me wings to fly and for the sacrifices you made so I could pursue my passion.

To my dear husband and three beautiful children, you make the journey all worth it.

To ALL my family, in laws and friends. You know I Love and appreciate you.

Finally, to God Almighty who graces me daily. Thank you for your many gifts and for loving me more than I love myself. I am like a fish out of water without you.

# DEDICATION

I dedicate this book to the future work force around the world who will not just work for a financial reward; but ensure they consciously build careers that create impact.

# TABLE OF CONTENT

SECTION ONE
# Introduction to Building A Conscious Career

## CHAPTER ONE

# There is No Magic Formula

*"The best way to predict the future is to create it"*
- **Peter Drucker**

Friday is perhaps the most exciting day of the average worker's week. You can see the glitter on the faces of employees as they count down to the close of business. Thank God It's Friday! Many workers cannot wait to throw off their jackets and catch the next parade to a place where they can cut themselves loose and enjoy every bit of life - the life that seems to evade them when they pick up their bags and files and head to work on Mondays.

For Florence, she just wanted to sleep. Her life was what many considered a dream; a young woman fast rising through the ranks and earning an enviable income. Unlike myriad stories that make the rounds in offices among the unemployed about women who achieved quick progress, she had reached the heights of her career purely based on merit. Florence works hard. She had joined the firm immediately after her service year and the company's executives had taken an interest in her unrivalled dedication and selfless service for the growth of the company. Due to her commitment, the company provided her with the required support she needed to move forward in her career faster. However, in the midst of the corporate clutter, progress reports and promotion news, Florence still felt a void inside of her, one she struggled to fill.

"I just have this feeling I could do more than this. Maybe not necessarily more, but I feel like there is something missing, something I should be doing that I am not," she told her friend, Kate, as she negotiated a bend on the road to her house.

"You know how we talked about changing the world when we leave school?" she paused to adjust her glasses and then returned her hand to the wheel.

"Where is all that now?" She continued.

"Don't get me wrong, I appreciate how much progress I am making. I want that too. Yet, I feel a widening disconnect between who I am and other things I want to be. Sometimes, I wish I could be like you. You know, have the liberty to do what I want. I barely even have time for myself."- **Kate giggled.**

She was both impressed and inspired by the subtle rings of compliments that Florence sometimes threw at her. You could see her cheeks sink into a dimple or as she welcomed those words. She needed them, a number of times, here and there. She, like Florence, had an admirable life. Unlike Florence, Kate founded her own initiative called 'The Kate Project', where she trains underprivileged women in marginalized communities in different skills in order to empower them to take charge of important decisions in their lives. Her heart glistened with joy at the progress she was making. She could not throw that life away. However, beneath that layer of joy, was another layer that was beginning to feel inadequate. While she did not wait until she was in her 40s or 50s to directly impact her community, she had begun to feel a void expand in her heart.

She wanted Florence's life too. Maybe not all of it, but the comfortable part – the part that had no financial worries. An extra bit of certainty that she could afford the life she loved while creating impact. Her fulfilment seemed aloof and that gap widened with the passing of each day. It is the reason why when she received compliments like the one Florence just threw at her, she embraced them and thought for a few minutes that perhaps, it was not that bad after all. That feeling did not last very long, however. It disappeared into a mist as they folded into girl's talk about some of the nice things they would love to get in a few months.

There are no easy pathways to building a fulfilling and rewarding career. The desire for a life of happiness and self-actualization is common in most human beings. In 1943, psychologist Abraham Maslow proposed in his paper, 'A Theory of Human Motivation' that humans go through different motivations at different stages of their lives. This was further expatiated in his subsequent paper, Motivation and Personality (1954). Maslow categorized human needs into two segments; Deficiency Needs and Growth Needs. Deficiency needs occurs due to deprivation while growth needs stem from the desire to grow as a person. Example of growth needs include hunger and safety needs. When people have considerably fulfilled their deficiency needs, they begin to seek to grow towards fulfilment.

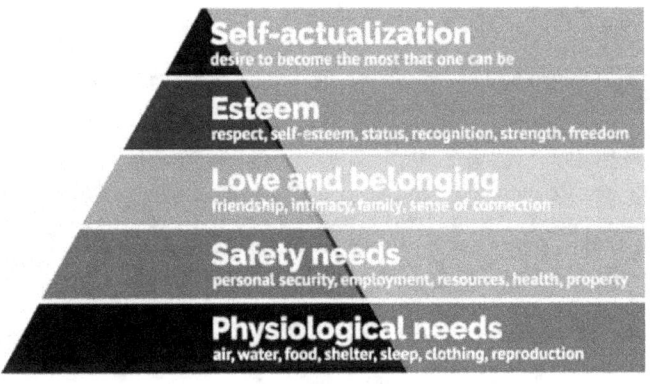

Figure 1 Source: https://www.simplypsychology.org/maslow.html

According to the hierarchy of needs, the highest order of motivation is self-actualization needs. In some expanded versions of Maslow's hierarchy of needs, this is upped by transcendence needs. Most notably, Maslow's research shared that people are motivated by specific needs and some needs take precedence over others.

You may be wondering, how does this book, focused on building careers, relate with fulfilling one's self-actualization needs? Self-actualization is about finding the utmost fulfilment in the things you do. It is about realizing your potential and reaching the peak of your experiences. Personal growth is critical to self-actualization and deriving fulfilment from your career is an example of attaining self-actualization. A career is an extension of us. Most times, we seek out a career in areas where we can be our best. Building a rewarding and fulfilling career is about getting the best out of our career, such that by the end of it, we believe we have reached the peak of our lives and attained maximum satisfaction in pursuing that career.

As we age, we want to look back on our lives and be delighted about the decisions we made. We also want to look forward and continue to grow in that path, chiseling away our inadequacies and maximizing our lives to the fullest potential.

You often hear people say these days, "Yes, I have a great job, but I feel like something is missing." What usually happens in such a situation is that the person believes she has no choice but to cling to her job. Several years afterwards, perhaps after her retirement or close to it, she goes on this wild spree of giving back to the society in a desperate attempt to catch up on lost years, where she feels she had bartered her dreams for money. In some other cases, a person might feel they have not explored the world enough because of several constraints they had been unable to control, or had little idea of how to maneuver. At the twilight of their career, such people begin to seek that fulfilment. Some are lucky to still find it, while others have to make do with anything they get at this point.

The alternative is when you hear people say, "I enjoy what I am doing, but I don't make a lot of money." While such persons get all the accolades for creating such defining impact on the lives of the people around them, they are unable to transfer that success to building a convenient life. Although they may be recipients of multiple monetary gifts, they have little control over the income that comes with running such passion projects. This leaves them financially deficient and they are often forced to settle for a different life.

You may have also heard in different conversations, that you usually have to choose between the life you admire and the one that pays your bills. There are those who tried to pursue having the job of their dreams with having the job that will pay their bills and they tried very hard to juggle both lives albeit with a lot of difficulty. Such people often opt for a high paying job while they make some time out to do some charity work on the side to satisfy their inner yearnings. While doing this is not bad, it is also not being intentional about your career. The good news is that you do not always have to choose between the two. This book is about helping you to make career choices that will not only allow you to live a happy and fulfilled life, but also make the money you require to meet your needs. As you read along, you will learn how to pursue the life of your dreams in a less difficult way.

One thing I have learnt is that different people have different things they want to achieve with their lives.

We cannot presume that everyone wants the same things that we do. However, I assume that if you are reading this book and are looking to find something meaningful in it, then you most likely are looking to have a fulfilling and rewarding career. I am happy to welcome you on this journey to finding yourself and setting yourself on the path to getting the best out of your career.

The advantage this book provides you is that it sets you up to make conscious career decisions and to take actions that will improve the outcome of your life. Whether or not you are just starting out in your career, in the middle of one, or you do not have a job at all, every point is a good starting point. A memorable quote about starting appears in the classic book, The Curious Case of Benjamin Button:

"For what it's worth...it's never too late, or in my case too early, to be whoever you want to be. There's no time limit. Start whenever you want. You can change or stay the same. There are no rules to this thing. We can make the best or the worst of it. I hope you make the best of it. I hope you see things that startle you. I hope you feel things you've never felt before. I hope you meet people who have a different point of view. I hope you live a life you're proud of, and if you're not, I hope you have the courage to start over again." — **F. Scott Fitzgerald**

It all begins with the decision to start or restart. It does not matter when you choose to take this decision. I recommend, the earlier, the better though. What comes first is the deliberate decision to make more meaning out of your life and put yourself in the right position to make the best of it. Building a fulfilling and rewarding career begins with the decision to take charge.

Are you ready to take charge of your career? Meditate on these questions and answer them as honestly as you can:

- What are the things that you currently feel you have no control over that defines your career growth?
- What things do you wish to change about your career?
- What kind of career do you aspire to have?
- How important are these aspirations to you?
- What do you wish to contribute to the world?
- If you have the power to do anything about your career, what decisions will you make?

## The Power of Intentionality

I learnt about the power of being intentional very early in my life. Getting to choose between the sciences and arts was perhaps my first chance at making a critical decision about my life. I was in JSS 3 and I believe it was an important decision that helped set me on the path to a fulfilling secondary school life. Our world is about patterns, mostly repeated across different fields and phases of our lives. My decision to choose arts ahead of the sciences came I studied who I was, what I liked to do, what brought me fulfilment and what I was best at doing. It laid the foundation to my career development. It also formed the basis of how I make important decisions that define my career.

Rather than decide based on the choices or preferences of others, I looked inwards. I loved music. I was part of a small music group with my friends and we had started to enjoy some fame in our neighbourhood. My time with my music group was one of the most enjoyable periods of my teenage years. I also discovered that I did not just enjoy music; the creative ability to connect with other people in a fun and exciting way also thrilled me. So I chose the arts.

The success of that decision reflected in my final exams. The few distinctions I got were in Government, History and Literature. In addition to this, I was made one of the school's Social Prefects in my final year. By the time I left secondary school, I knew I made the right decision, which did not only feel fulfilling throughout the journey, but was ultimately rewarding.

Thus, the first step to a fulfilling and rewarding career is to understand yourself. You need to ask yourself these questions:

Who am I? – A common mistake people make is to define themselves according to their profession, location or education. All those things are acquired. When you ask yourself this question, your answer should be independent of the place you lived, the school you attended and the job you are currently doing. It should be a reflection of your personality, your likes and dislikes, what is valuable to you, what is not and so on. What defines your identity? While the question, 'Who am I', continues to be one of the most difficult questions a person can be faced with, especially since humans are a spectrum of identities; you can begin to figure out the answer by acknowledging some of the traits that are apparent to you or surface more frequently than others do. Other questions you should ask alongside this important question are;

- What do I like doing?
- What motivates me?
- What things do I easily excel at doing?
- What are my weaknesses?
- What makes me happy?
- What bothers me?
- What are my biggest goals?
- What are my immediate goals?
- If I had no constraint, what decisions will I make?

This process is called Self Awareness. Some others call it Self Discovery. Too many people are so caught up in the activities of their daily lives that they forget to take a step back and re-examine their own lives. Just like working in your business and working on your business are two different things, it is important for you to pause in order to take a deeper look at yourself and find out everything about you and your current state. Are you happy with yourself?

When you begin to understand yourself, you can make decisions that improve your life and move you towards fulfilment. You will know what things to accept and what things to reject. You can decide which events to attend and which you should turn down. You can determine what opportunities will move you closer to your goals and which will only waste your time. In essence, you can begin to choose the direction your life takes through the decisions you make. More importantly, you can begin to do this consciously. Questions about your decisions can come before you make them, rather than as an afterthought or during regrets. An evergreen poem Invictus by William Ernest Henley reads,

It matters not how strait the gate, How charged with punishments the scroll, I am the master of my fate, I am the captain of my soul.

By answering these questions and with the help of this book, you will be positioned to take charge of your career. In addition, you will get the guidance you need to attain the career of your dreams despite the challenges that may abound.

### Discovering Yourself
There are several tools you may use to discover who you are. Some are more accurate than the others. However, the accuracy is not the most important. What matters is that these tools help you to understand yourself much better than you probably did before you used them. As a result, you should use these tools as part of your journey to self-discovery, but also rely more on your inner truths to help you find yourself.

### SWOT
SWOT is the acronym for Strength, Weakness, Opportunities and Threats. This is simply doing an assessment of yourself by stating clearly what your strengths and weaknesses are. Your opportunities are those things which you can take advantage of to become even more successful while your threats are the things that pose a disadvantage to you, which you must find a way to end so you can be more successful.

Your threats are those things that can stop you from achieving your goals. Doing a SWOT analysis helps you to understand the positive and negative sides of you, so that you can harness them to become a better person. This is akin to doing a self-appraisal.

Examples of questions you may ask yourself are these:

Strength
What am I good at?
What services can I offer?
What resources do I possess?
What skills do I have?
What positive personalities do I have?

Weakness
What am I not-so-good at?
What do I need to learn?
What negative personalities do I have?
What frightens me?
What causes me to fail?

Opportunities
Who can help me become better?
What accessible beneficial programmes can I take advantage of now?
What alternatives do I have to reach my goals?
What resources do I have access to that will move me closer to my goals?
What education do I need to attain to reach my goals?
Threats
What challenges do I have that can stop me from reaching my goals?
Who are my competitors/ who can stop me from reaching my goals?
What new trend do I need to learn?

**TEMPERAMENT TEST**
This is a simple test, which is also useful to help you understand yourself better. It classifies individuals across four personalities. These are Sanguine, Choleric, Melancholic and Phlegmatic.

These terms were coined by Aelius Galenus, a Greek physician, who based it on the four fundamental bodily humours which, according to Ancient Greek theory, determines the state of health of people.

You can take this test on https://openpsychometrics.org/tests/O4TS, an Open Source Psychometrics Project developed in 2014 by Eric Jorgenson.

### PERSONALITY TEST

The personality test helps you to assess your individual traits that are germane to the kind of decisions you make and how you view the world. They usually consist of a set of questions that you have to answer. Your answers are compiled and used in the process of personality selection where your type of person is determined across a variety of personality scales. One of the most popular personality type indicators used across the world is the Myers-Briggs Type Indicator.

If you must take a personality test such as Myers-Briggs Type Indicator, you must be brutally honest when filling the questionnaire. You should understand that if you choose ideal answers, instead of answers that truly describe who you are, as you know yourself, then you will be kicking off this exercise on the wrong foot and it may not be able to help you.

To take a personality test, one site I recommend is https://www.16personalities.com/free-personality-test. Here, you can take a free test and get a deeper insight into who you are. You may also get to see people who are like you, and who reached the peak of their careers.

By the time you have completed each of these processes, you will see yourself through a clearer lens. I believe that this introspection is the best place to start as you move towards attaining fulfilment in your career. When we understand where we are, then we can learn how to move towards our destination; where we want to be. You see, a person is said to be lost when they do not know their current location, which usually makes it very difficult to move in the direction of their destination.

When a person can find her coordinates, then she can do all that is necessary to move towards her destination.

Congratulations, if you have gone through the steps above and you have taken a self-inventory! It means you are ready to take the next step in building a fulfilling and rewarding career. If you have not, it is important for you to you do this before you move on to the next chapter.

SECTION TWO

# Introduction to Building A Conscious Career

CHAPTER TWO

# Career Paths

*"Either I will find a way or I will make one"*
**-Philip Sidney**

Remember Florence from the previous chapter? She could not get the conversation she had with Kate out of her mind. This was not the first time issues regarding her career were on the front burner and occupying the top spot in her thoughts. One part of her wanted to be certain she was not just being impatient, and the other part wanted to be sure she knew and had weighed all her options. Even if she decided to make changes, what kind of changes could she make? What were her options? A few times, here and there, she found herself looking out for opportunities. Would she need to make an early switch in her career or could she attain fulfilment in her current path? She asked herself many questions as she continued to dig for answers. Many employees eventually get to a point where they evaluate their career; Florence had reached that point already.

Kate's worries were a little different. At one time or the other, she had felt her passion wane. She felt she was burning out and might soon let go. While she enjoyed what she was doing, she felt incomplete and wished she could take a break. Perhaps, she could seek out new adventures. One thing she was certain about was that she loved her work enough to be able to go on; she just needed ideas on how to maximize her passion for it. In addition to this, she wanted to ensure she was taking full advantage of the path she took.

Both Florence and Kate sought ways to make the best of their careers. Let me put a note of caution here; this book does not provide a bespoke solution to Florence or Kate's problems. Rather, it is a guide which is based on my experience, the experiences of people I know and those who many of you also know and look up to, backed by years of research. I had to study extensively in order to build a career that makes me proud and I am convinced that if you carefully read along, you will discover important pointers that will help you to build a conscious career that is fulfilling and rewarding.

A career is a lifelong activity. Often, people use the word 'career', as a synonym for words like vocation, occupation, work or profession. Knowing that you will spend most of your life working makes it an important part of your life and you should aim to not only get it right, but also enjoy it. This is not too much to ask. While a career is what a person does to earn a living, I believe a career also defines you eventually; who you are and possibly who you become. Think about Oprah Winfrey, and what comes to mind is her success in the talk show industry. Take away that career from Oprah, and you find yourself scrambling for a definition. Perhaps, if you were a member of her family or in her close circle, you might know her differently. However, if you are as successful as Oprah is in your career, it becomes difficult to take away that part of your life from your identity.

For some people who have old relatives that served in the army, you find neighbours calling such relatives "old soldier". Let me be more practical. There is a very good chance you saved many of your acquaintances' contacts on your phone with their professions or place of work attached to their names. While people do this for easy identification, it is also noteworthy that a person's career is quite important and eventually forms part of their identity as perceived by other people and the person herself. So why should you not be more vested in building that part of your life? Why should you leave it to chance?

The success of your career speaks volumes about you in circles beyond your close network. It may inspire those in your community or even millions of other people you may never get to meet. Your work life is also where you are most active as a human. You are more fit, psychologically and physically, than you are in other phases of your life. You definitely want to spend that period of your life making the best out of life.

I will not be addressing all kinds of careers in this book. There are actually thousands of career possibilities out there. Instead, I will focus on the different ways you can pursue your career, in whatever field you choose. I assume that if you are reading this book, you are currently about to pursue or are pursuing a career already in a certain field.

You must be conscious about the career choices you make. A conscious career is one where the individual deliberately plans and commits to having a thriving career. Normally, people commit to having careers that positively affect the lives of others and are rewarding as well. When I was about to choose my course of study at the university, I already had in mind the kind of career I wanted to have. Therefore, it was relatively easy for me to choose a course that would set me on the path to the career I wanted. One thing I wish to say, however, is that choosing the course I wanted to study was not straightforward. I applied unsuccessfully to a Federal University to study International Relations and Mass Communication. My parents then suggested I applied to a private university just starting out in the country at the time and I did. At this point, none of the courses I chose earlier were available and I had to choose a different course. This time, I opted for Political Science and Public Administration.

What made this easy for me is very important and I will share with you. I clearly understood what my passion was, and I had made the distinction between my passion and my career. When you are able to make this distinction, it will become very easy for you to go in the path of your passion in whatever field you find yourself. While some passions are more specific than others, people can generally fulfil their purposes in different fields. Once you acknowledge this, you will become flexible in your career pursuit. You will also become unstoppable, because wherever you find yourself, you will be able to shoot for glory and express your passion.

## WHAT IS THE DIFFERENCE BETWEEN YOUR PASSION AND YOUR CAREER—

Your passion is in your values. It is the person you are. Your passion is what you want to offer the world. Usually, your passion builds on your strengths. For example, I may be passionate about making the world a cleaner place or ending poverty. For some people, their passion is to ensure there is justice in the world or to bring prosperity to their communities. Your passion can be anything.

One thing you should note is that the less you tie your passion to a particular profession, the more options you will have of expressing that passion. Remember, in Chapter 1 when I shared how to define who you are. I indicated that it is important that you do not define yourself by your location, education or profession.

You should try to define your passion outside career options. This is not to say that you cannot be passionate about a particular career. You just have to ensure you make this decision after proper consideration. For example, if my passion is to end poverty in my country, I may do this as a farmer who caters to people's food needs. I may do this through empowerment trainings. I may do this by becoming a politician who makes favourable policies. I may do this by creating jobs. In the end, if you choose any of these career paths or are left with certain career options, you can still find a way to express your passion and be fulfilled at the end of your career. Therefore, you should always strive to define your passion outside your career.

Life is exciting when you can explore many options and still fulfil your purpose. You will enjoy more freedom in the pursuit of happiness. But, if your passion is defined by a particular career option, this is good too. For example, you may want to be a humanitarian nurse. Perhaps you do not only care about tending to the sick or wounded; you feel you will only find fulfilment if you tend to sick and wounded people in war-torn or emergency areas. It means you are dedicated to attaining fulfilment only through this career path. While this narrows your options, it also makes you more focused in reaching your peak in that career. Focus is a powerful thing when used appropriately. My advice is, when your passion is defined by a particular career, ensure that you have carefully studied yourself and have discovered that you may only find fulfilment through that particular path.

Your career is like a vessel through which you express your passion. You may go through different careers while fulfilling your passion. For instance, you may have the passion for football. But in pursuing your passion, you may have a footballing career, then a coaching career, then a football administration career and eventually become an investor in the business of football. You may even own a clinic to help footballers remain fit. Or you could end up in the technology side of football, producing digital games or technologies used in advancing the footballing game. Thus, your passion through any of these careers may be for football, but you would have successfully demonstrated your passion in any of these fields above.

Understanding the difference between your passion and your career makes it less difficult to choose a career. Ensure you can clearly connect the dots between your career of choice and your passion.

When I had to choose new courses that were different from the ones I had chosen earlier when I applied to the Federal University, it was much easier. All I had to do was try to see what courses among the available options could help me express my passion and fulfil my purpose, same thing the unavailable course would have allowed me to do. I knew I wanted to make a difference and change the world. This was my mantra at that time. In addition to understanding my passion, whatever course I chose also had to be related to the fields I enjoyed.

## MORE REASONS WHY THIS IS IMPORTANT

In our fast moving world, jobs fade out very quickly. Certain jobs that you know now may no longer be available in a few years. Some courses of study may lose relevance in society. What will you do when this happens? Will you remain stuck in the past? The jobs you know now may not be available tomorrow, and the jobs that do not currently exist will surface. As new technologies are deployed and new discoveries made, our world will keep evolving and those who do not adapt to it will quickly fade out or be left to bite the dust. You do not want to be among those who are unable to adapt to new trends.

According to Charles Darwin, "It is not the strongest of the species that survives, nor the most intelligent, but the one most responsive to change." Your ability to adapt your passion to your career and the changing times will put you at an advantage to make the most out of your career. The conscious decision to thrive wherever you find yourself is the true trait of champions.

Twenty years ago, you could barely find any job role called Social Media Manager, or Search Engine Optimization expert. Today, we have these roles. Certain jobs are fading out as well, while some jobs remain but are executed in new ways. All of this shows that while your passion will remain, it is quite possible for you to express it in different ways as you grow or as the world evolves.

One thing I ensure I do is follow innovation to be on top of any new trends in my profession. Once I notice a new trend, I am an early adopter, wanting to know more about it and how to take action and use it to my advantage.

## CATEGORIES OF CAREERS

Let us look at the different ways you may pursue a career. While this list is not conclusive, we find that most careers fall under these categories.

### 1.    EMPLOYMENT/ INTERNSHIP

This refers to working for an individual, an entity or an organization, in return for compensation. This is perhaps where the largest category of people's careers will fall. Many times, this is where people begin their careers. Whether you choose to be a doctor or a writer, chances are you will be paid by an organization at one point or another in your career to provide this service. Hence, you are a provider of labour. Interns, however, are more inclined to gaining experience in a chosen field with little or no pay attached to it.

### 2.    ENTREPRENEURSHIP

Entrepreneurs are people who start their own ventures and are thus employers of labour. They create avenues where people can exchange value. They make the decisions that affect the organization in which they work and usually provide the direction for the whole organization. Usually, such organizations are based on the ideas and values of the founder. Social entrepreneurs are people who start their own ventures for social or public good.

### 3.    VOLUNTEERING

Volunteering is lending yourself to a cause, whether it is paid or voluntary. Volunteering is similar to employment, except it is a bit more flexible. Unlike in employment, the goal of a volunteer is to advance a cause as opposed to providing a service in exchange for a reward. As we go further, I will delve deeper into how volunteering can be a critical tool in fulfilling your purpose, and how it has played a big role in moving me closer to the peak of my career.
While you have a lot of people who give out their time and skills to a

cause, some of the more famous ones include Mother Theresa and Bono.

### 4.   LEARNING

Some people commit themselves to a life of learning. These people are interested either in learning about the world's history or in advancing the frontiers of human knowledge. They go wherever they can to acquire more knowledge in their chosen field. While learners may be paid as employees, most times, they get support through grants, sponsorships and donations. Famous people who dedicated their lives to learning are Nikola Tesla, Clay Christensen, Albert Einstein, Aristotle, Archimedes, Galileo Galilei, Thomas Edison, Marie Curie and Leonardo da Vinci.

### 5.   ACTIVISM/ADVOCACY

You may choose a career where your role is prompting others into action towards a cause.

Activists usually take different routes to ensure change in the society. However, rather than allow processes take their course, activists want to speed up the action or in cases where nothing is done at all, seek to command action. Famous activists include Ken Saro Wiwa, Martin Luther King, Nelson Mandela, Malcolm X, Funmilayo Ransome Kuti, Mahatma Ghandi and Rosa Parks.

### 6.   INVESTOR / PHILANTHROPIST /SPONSOR

People who invest usually have enough money or resources to make things work for them. An investor is one who commits her resources, rather than labour to an organization, project, cause or product. One can choose to fulfil one's passion by supporting those who are working in fields that directly help fulfil that purpose. For example, if my goal is to end hunger, instead of trying to create a solution for that, I can put my resources behind those who are already working to solve that problem. If these people make significant progress in ending hunger, then I can say that I am pursuing my passion of ending hunger. Some famous investors and philanthropists include Warren Buffet, Bill Gates and Mark Zuckerberg.

When you choose a particular career, chances are high that they fall under one or more of these five categories. If your passion is to save lives, you may either work as a doctor in a hospital (employee), start your own hospital (entrepreneur), volunteer at the Red Cross (Volunteering), study how people can cure malaria (learning), agitate towards the proper remuneration of doctors (activism) or provide resources for people who are saving lives to amplify their impact (investor).

## QUICK EXERCISE
Choose a particular passion and see how you may express that passion across these different categories. Try this exercise with your passion and other examples as well.

---

**MEDITATION POINT**

If the job I currently do no longer exists, are there other ways in which I can follow my passion?

---

One thing you should know is that you can attain fulfilment expressing your passion within any of these options. Some people even transition from one category to another. You may also find people who go through all the categories as they continue to find new ways to attain fulfilment without letting go of their passion. Suddenly, you find that you have many options to build a career. If you get it right, all of these categories can be financially rewarding as well as fulfilling. You do not have to make a trade off.

For every one person who went directly to start their businesses after school, there are many others who were first employees, then business owners. Most times, people who are investors have either worked in major establishments as employees or have owned their own businesses.

Take Florence and Kate for example. While Florence is an employee, Kate floats her own initiative and controls the decisions that affect that initiative. If Florence wishes, she could start her own initiative after working for a few years in the corporate world. Another thing Florence could do is to volunteer at an initiative of her choice, perhaps during weekends or at initiatives that allow her to contribute remotely. Florence could also look at is what is known as Intrapreneurship. Often, people believe they have to switch careers before they can fulfil their purpose or contribute to the advancement of humanity. This is not always true. One thing I have explored while trying to build my career is look at how I can achieve my goals within the construct of wherever I find myself. The first thing is not to consider leaving, but rather to ensure you have no other options in your current establishment. This should be the major reason why you would leave an organization, especially one that supports you appropriately.

## So what is Intrapreneurship—

Although it is a relatively new concept, intrapreneurship simply means acting like an entrepreneur but within an established business or organization. Intrapreneurs lead innovation within an organization. They use insights and trends that they have gathered to create new products or services. Although intrapreneurs may still be governed by the rules of the organization, they have liberty and much more support in the pursuit of innovation. Like entrepreneurs, intrapreneurs take risks and find efficient ways to accomplish tasks. Most importantly, they provide solutions for problems that yields profit for their organization.

Therefore, if Florence is seeking new ways to express her passion to change the world, and feels like her current role does not allow her do that, she may create a new initiative and share it with her company's management. If she is able to articulate it properly along with the vision of the company and also define how the initiative will bring value to the company, she may get a chance to start expressing her passion without the insecurities that come with starting afresh. More often than not, companies are seeking new ideas to remain relevant in the industry.

This is even more so when there is neck break competition with other companies in the same industry. Companies will usually invest in initiatives that give them an edge and also return value. Thus, when you are able to introduce such initiatives that excite you as well as deliver value to your company, you hit a homerun.

## UNDERSTANDING THE WORLD OF WORK

Our world is constantly changing. The speed at which this is now happening is incredible. This is because the rate at which technology and information now advances is much faster than decades ago. In the near future, the speed will rise exponentially. This means that while many fields will remain, several jobs will fall off the log.

One thing to also note is that the rate at which people switch across different roles has also increased. The average person may occupy up to eight different roles before the end of her career.
Sometimes, these roles are not directly related to one another. One factor that influences switching roles is people's continued efforts to attain the right work/life balance in their lives. Other times, it could be situations such as moving to a new home, marriage and raising children, or acquiring new education or skills.

When you begin to understand how things operate, you will put yourself at an advantage to take charge of the opportunities in your career. This includes understanding what employers demand, if you pursue a career as an employee. It also means learning what it takes to run a business, if you decide to be an entrepreneur.

When you have carefully gone through these meditation questions, I trust that you will have a clearer perspective of your career. You do not need to beat yourself up for not knowing these things before now. Careers always involve lifelong learning. Submitting yourself to learning, relearning and discovery puts you on the path to building a conscious career.

There are different activities that may contribute to building your career. This includes:

i)        Education. Perhaps, this is the most direct way to prepare for and grow your career. While a lot of people eventually venture into careers that are unrelated to their course of study in university, it does not take away from the fact that their learning contributed to the kind of ideas they were able to bring to the table. Further education in areas where you now practice will more often than not make your goals more achievable and within a shorter time frame. Quality education gives you an important leverage for great achievement. It gives you the freedom to do the impossible, to reach the peak of your potentials and be the best you can be. It is important for you to enroll for new courses as you grow in your career, that is if you intend to consciously build a fulfilling and rewarding career. The sayings of Nelson Mandela and Maya Angelou succinctly captures the value of education.

"Education is the most powerful weapon which you can use to change the world." —**Nelson Mandela**

"I did then what I knew how to do. Now that I know better, I do better." —**Maya Angelou**

ii)        Community activities: By virtue of the fact that we live in a society and humans are social beings, relationships with people in our community often lead to a person's commitment to a few duties that will help move that community forward. Such experiences may eventually translate to a useful addition to your portfolio and help advance your career.

iii)        Internships: This is an important avenue for you to work and learn in a profession before fully venturing into it. Although internships are beginning to appear as an alternative to jobs for some people, depending on the situation of the country they find themselves. However, several organizations and people still approach internship the right way.

iv)        Volunteer work: I am so positive about the value volunteering adds to your career that I have taken out a whole chapter to talk about it and how you may maximize it for your own career as well. Volunteering gives you as much value as you are willing to give your time and effort to it consciously.

v)        Leisure activities: What you do in your free time tells on your career. While I encourage that you spend your leisure time decompressing and participating in activities that help you relax and socialise, to become more productive eventually, you will have to commit some of your leisure time to doing something that aids self-improvement e.g. learning a new skill, new language, reading etc. According to Benjamin Franklin;

"Leisure is the time for doing something useful. This leisure the diligent person will obtain the lazy one never."

vi)     Employment: Your present and previous employment contribute massively to your career. Since your job is what you invest your time and skill doing daily, if you are properly committed to these jobs, you will most likely have become better in several areas of your professional journey.

vii)     Enterprise activities: When you engage in initiatives that seek to add value to the organization you are part of beyond the scope of your role in that company, you improve yourself. Some of these activities may have occurred as you try to put to practical use knowledge you have about the external business environment or ways you have explored to create value as a service or product.

viii)     Trainings: Going for trainings to augment your formal education is a great way to lead a fulfilling career. Whether you're trying to expand your knowledge of your profession or you want to get acquainted with new trends, the right training gives you a leg up and can significantly move you closer to the peak of your career.

ix)     Discussions: Discussions range from those conversations you have with your colleagues to the ones that happen online or within august gatherings. The quality of the conversations you have will eventually tell on your career. When you understand this, you will not waste your time engaging in conversations that barely add anything to you.

x)     Reading: The kind of books you read has a great influence on the quality of your decisions. Reading is not only limited to books. Articles, journals, online and offline posts and so on are some other examples of what should form your reading focus. The goal of reading is to expand your knowledge, especially in your chosen field or fields. Reading, when done judiciously, gives you the opportunity not to make the same mistakes as others who have done similar things as you are doing.

"The more that you read, the more things you will know. The more that you learn, the more places you'll go." — **Dr. Seuss.**

While building a conscious career, all these different activities are important pieces that lead you to the peak of your career when you approach them judiciously.

## TYPES OF JOBS BASED ON DURATION

**FULL TIME** – These jobs require the full commitment of employees throughout a calendar year, except during vacations. The amounts of time commitment organizations require from their full time employees differ. However, many employees commit between 40 - 60 hours every week to their organizations. Usually, full time employees have to be at their place of work during working hours.

**PART TIME** – A person who works part time commits only a specific period within a week to render her service to the employer. Part time jobs usually require a person's presence during the time which she has committed to that job. A part time job may range between 10 - 20 hours a week.

**INTERNSHIP** – A person who enrols as an intern aims to use the job as a platform to learn more about the occupation. Interns cut across undergraduate students and graduate students. Some people also use internships as a pre-engagement to securing a full time job at an organiation.

**SEASONAL JOBS** – Seasonal employment is only available at specific times of the year. Beyond these periods, such jobs are not available and only return when the season comes around again.

**REMOTE JOBS** – These types of jobs afford you the opportunity to work away from the employing organization and in your own place of choice. Remote jobs are usually available for roles that require minimal contact between the employee and the employer without significantly jeopardizing the quality and quantity of work to be delivered.

**CONTRACT JOBS –** These jobs are mostly on demand. A person gains employment periodically when her service is required. When she completes her work, her contract is terminated. People who work on contract, in some cases, also have the ability to work on several projects simultaneously.

## TYPES OF CAREERS BASED ON INDUSTRY

While I won't be able to showcase all the kinds of careers that exist, the list below includes a comprehensive number. These are different industries in which people may pursue careers.

· Agriculture, Food and Natural Resources
· Architecture and Construction
· Arts, Media and Communication
· Business Management and Administration
· Education and Training
· Finance
· Government and Public Administration
· Healthcare Science
· Hospitality and Tourism
· Human (Social) Services
· Information Technology
· Law, Public Safety, and Security
· Manufacturing
· Marketing, Sales, and Services
· Science, Technology, and Engineering
· Transportation, Distribution and Logistics
· General Labour
· Retail and Commerce

I have provided this list to give an overview of the different ways careers may be segmented and to bring into perspective, especially for this book, the different paths through which you may choose to pursue your career. Although there are different careers that you may pursue at different stages of your life, the important thing is your ability to connect it with your passion or anything that makes you feel you are fulfilling your purpose. As I highlighted earlier, your career is different from your passion. In the following chapter, I will delve more into finding, understanding and utilizing your passion as you seek to build a fulfilling and rewarding career.

## CHAPTER THREE

# Channelling Your Passion for your Career

*"Passion is what gives meaning to our lives.*
*It's what allows us to achieve success beyond*
*our wildest imagination.*
*Try to find a career path that you have a passion for."*
**-Henry Samueli**

In the last chapter, I mentioned briefly how important it is to find your passion and ensure your career connects with that passion. In this chapter, we will continue by taking a further look into what passion is and how you may create a conscious career by deliberately engaging in areas where you can express your passion.

In order to draw a more relatable picture on the need to identify one's passion, let's examine the curious cases of Kate and Florence, two friends who are exploring ways to maximize their passion.

## KATE'S DILEMMA

If you re-examine Kate's story, you may find that while she loved her work, she felt she was not getting the most out of herself or her career. As a person who was passionate about helping underprivileged women in her society, she was certain she was doing what she loved; except with time, she soon found out that a lot of other things were just as important. She was sometimes worried that she was not exploring a great deal of the opportunities that were available to her. There were times when she tired out and was uninterested in her work for many days. Whenever she reached this point, she wondered if it was normal for her to lose interest in her work and hoped to learn more about what to do when she burns out, especially to remain passionate. Kate wanted to understand her passion more and discover how best to channel it into a fulfilling and rewarding career.

## FLORENCE'S DILEMMA

Florence's dilemma was that she loved her job. More than anything, it afforded her a good life. She worked in a good company that promised her growth across her career. She had access to several networks that were quite beneficial to her success. Yet, she felt she could reach a greater level of fulfilment than she already did. One thing she knew was that happiness was a journey rather than a destination. While her job had the capacity to put her at an enviable career position upon retirement, she felt the need to enjoy that happiness daily instead. If she truly loved her work, it should give her fulfilment at the end of each day. She should not be happy only when her company credited her bank account with salaries and allowances or when she got the chance to take a break from her work. You should be happy to go to work every day because you are doing what you love.

Happiness is not something you postpone for the future; it is something you design for the present.
- **Jim Rohn.**

From careful examination, you will discover that both of them felt there was a gaping void and they were desperate to fill it. A lot of times, this does not depend on how committed you are to your work, or how much patience or perseverance you have had to endure. Maximizing your passion requires a different level of acknowledgement – an acknowledgement that explores your roles and ensures that it has been properly setup to make you fulfilled daily.

Building a conscious career that is fulfilling will require that you work on something that makes you happy. According to Oprah Winfrey, "Work that you love gives you energy rather than exhaust you."

## HOW TO FIND YOUR PASSION

"Your work is going to fill a large part of your life, and the only way to be truly satisfied is to do what you believe is great work. And the only way to do great work is to love what you do. If you haven't found it yet, keep looking. Don't settle. As with all matters of the heart, you'll know when you find it. And, like any great relationship, it just gets better and better as the years roll on. So keep looking until you find it. Don't settle." - **Steve Jobs**

Many of us hear this every now and then: Follow Your Passion. Perhaps, you have heard it from friends, at a lecture, over the radio or during a session with a counsellor (or someone who acts like one). Even you want to do something in line with your passion, especially since you have been told it would ensure you enjoy your work.

36

Your passion is simply what you love doing. It is usually something you look forward to do and mostly at any time. It would not matter if you were rewarded for it or not, since engaging in that activity is enough reward for you. You are happy and fulfilled when operating in your passion. This is not to say that it does not involve hard work by the way.

I advise many people to follow their passion because that is what I do. However, people have met me with questions like, 'How do I find my passion?" and "How do I know if I have found my passion?"

I think for the second question, the answer is quite straightforward. You will know you have found your passion when you do work that makes you happy. You are excited by every chance to do that work. It does not have to come easily to you; you just need to have enough drive and conviction to go after that work. You are willing to learn and make sacrifices just to get the chance to do that work. When you finally get to the work, you are happy and say to yourself, this is me! It just feels right. When doing work that you love, at that time, you do not feel you should be doing anything else in the world.

One exercise I do is to ask myself; if I had no money worries, what will I spend most of my time working on? The reason this question is important is that, while our earnings or the remuneration attached to each job motivate many of us, when a job is built on passion, the job matters more to us beyond the remuneration. The chance to do awesomely well in that job is just as motivating as the reward we attain for doing it.

Take some minutes to ruminate over the following questions;

- If I had no financial worries, what will I spend the rest of your life doing?
- Which goals will I go after, if I had enough money to pursue anything?
- What work do I love doing with little hesitation?
- What work do I love doing that I always look forward to do?

One more reason to ask yourself that question is; it is quite possible to fulfil your passion in some other ways aside from your job. I will discuss this part later in this chapter.

For those who are yet to find their passion, here is a list of things you can do to point you to it. I must also say that patience is key to finding your passion. If you cannot point to it now, give it time.

### 1.    What work makes you happy—

You may increasingly find that I am quite particular about work. There are many things that can make you happy. The aim of this book is to help you find that work that falls in line with your happiness and more, help you make the decision to pursue it consciously to the peak

Thus, if you already have an answer to this, then you may be closer to finding your passion than you think. Secondly, you may end up with a list of jobs that make you happy. What you do in this case is to find a way to narrow it down to a single option – that work that sets your heart on fire and makes you extremely excited when you make progress in it.

## 2.   What were your Childhood Interests—

A way people find out what they love is to look back at what they enjoyed doing when they were young. Try to remember some of the activities you enjoyed. This helps because at that time, you were more at liberty to do what you love, and were not under the pressure to fend for yourself or others.

Although I acknowledge that as kids, our passion often switched from one career to another, depending on which we were exposed to for long. Therefore, as you go memory cruising, ensure you can highlight which interests actually got your blood running, and which were quite ephemeral. You should also check if you are still interested in those things before you conclude on which activities are likely to form your passion.

As a kid, I liked music. More importantly, I liked to express myself in any way I was comfortable with. I was very sociable and communicated freely with my friends. This is the reason it felt natural to pursue careers in the arts as opposed to the sciences.

## 3.   What Do You Love To Talk About—

If there is any field that gets you excited, you will love to talk about it. When topics from these fields are the subject of discussion, your interest becomes keen and you want to be part of the conversation. When you do not know much, you are also keen to learn more about that field and sometimes, are even willing to tell people about it.

This is something you love to go on and on about. It could be a problem you are passionate about fixing, or a field that excites you in a way that makes you desire to contribute to its growth. It is not only something you like to talk about, but one you are willing to spend your energy and money doing, if required. Your interest may also be your passion in that field and your ability to communicate that passion may just be your contribution to it.

## 4.    What Are You Good at Doing—

What talents do you have? A good way to answer this is to take an inventory of your natural skills. These skills may be things you have learnt over a period of time and continue to get better at. You can also identify which of these skills you use frequently and are eager to use when you are unable to use them.

## 5.    What Kind of Compliments Do You Receive from Friends, Acquaintances and Colleagues—

Another way to help you discover what you are good at doing is paying attention to compliments. When people send compliments your way, you may notice some similarities in what they praise you for doing. You can note some of these compliments in a journal and after having a collection of them, check for some consistency. It may also give you a broader view on some of the things you do very well that you do not notice. Examine all qualities people say you have, and work your way to the ones that most excite you.

## 6.    What Infuriates You—

Our soul can be set on fire in two different ways; one is what makes us extremely excited, and the other is what makes us extremely angry. More often than not, when things are wrong with the things we care deeply about, it infuriates us. Another cause for bitterness are problems we care deeply about, and having them around consistently leave us dissatisfied.

One of the things that led Kate to start The Kate Project was that she was dissatisfied with the marginalization and oppression that many underprivileged women consistently faced especially because they had no financial independence and often did not complete basic education.

7.    **What People Do I Admire and What Kind Of Work Do They Do—**

An interesting way to find your passion is to list out the people you admire and then list out the work each of them does or did. Why this is important is, even when we are unable to follow a certain path, we consciously or subconsciously admire people who are able to take that path and excel in it.

For example, if you find out that many of your favourite people are doctors, then you might want to consider what you have for the medical profession.

8.    **Explore and Experiment.**

More likely, there are different levels of enthusiasm to exploring career options at different phases of your life. One might be more willing to experiment at the start of a career than at the middle of it due to our gradual keenness on stability as we grow. However, a good way to stumble on your passion is to try your hands on several things until you find that which makes your soul glow. Be flexible in how you pursue your passion.

A less risky method to explore different ideas is volunteering. When you are not working, you can sign up to volunteer in one organization or the other. Such organizations might have roles that align with your core desires or not but you can explore within a structure. Thus, joining an organization can help you identify some of your attributes or interests.

9.    **Ask Friends for Advice.**

If you have been careful with choosing your friends, then this option will provide you with great insight into your passion. Your friends know you very well and know what kind of things you have done together in the past that left you scampering for more. They know what makes you glow and things you consciously can go on and on about. They are also aware of the things you are terrible at doing.

This information makes them first hand helpers at deciding where your passion lies. Consult them!

## 10. Be Patient.

For some people, they need time to conclude on what actually makes their heart tick. Sometimes, the only reason we do not find something is because we were never looking for it in the first place. Therefore, now that you have made a conscious decision to identify where your passion lies, you should not also rush it. Continue with your current activities, explore, be ready to try new things. Document those things that excite or infuriate you and review them periodically. Don't put pressure under yourself. This quote summarises passion:

"Your true passion should feel like breathing; it's that natural." ?
**Oprah Winfrey**

## MAKING YOUR PASSION INTO YOUR CAREER

The major essence of the journey to finding your passion is to help you connect it with your career. If your passion can be something as powerful as we have described earlier, then it makes sense to do work where you can express that passion. This is even more important in helping you stay focused and interested. When you are able to merge your passion with the work you do, or do work that you are passionate about, you live your best, feel fulfilled and it rewards you financially if cultivated properly. This is because, not only do you enjoy what you are doing, you are doing work you are willing to give your all for. When you give your 100 percent to your work, there is only one way you will travel, and that way is up! The best way to reach the peak of your career is to give it your best, and that is mostly possible when your work has your focus.

One person who I admire a lot is Oprah Winfrey, who incidentally is one of the most successful women in the world. At 22, Oprah held a well-paying job as a news reporter at a local media station. Due to a reshuffle within the organization, she was taken off her role. She eventually got a role in a talk show at the same local media station.

When she resumed work as a co-anchor on the programme called People Are Talking, she revealed at the Oprah After the Show programme, that the work just felt right for her. According to Winfrey, at her earlier job as a newscaster, before she came to realize her passion for the talk show business, she usually felt exhausted after each day of work. However, as soon as she got to anchor talk shows, she felt a different level of energy that drove her each day. Rather than having her work weigh her down repeatedly, it inspired her and gave her more energy to pursue it.

Oprah went from that point of being a co-host of a local talk show to the peak of the talk show industry. She was so successful that she also became the richest black woman in the world. She had managed a career that was both fulfilling and ultimately financially rewarding. Her journey to the top began when she finally found her passion. Incidentally, she found that passion while working her normal job in a local media station. However, because she had always had the right attitude to work and put her efforts into her normal work, when her company presented her with the opportunity to co-anchor a talk show, she was willing to give it a go. About ten years later, Oprah had her own talk show, the Oprah Winfrey Show, and had become the highest-rated talk show personality in America. When she would recount her experience, she said,

"If you can find what is your passion, if you find what you love, you never get tired. And if you get tired, you are refilled by the energy of your work." – **Oprah Winfrey.**

Unlike Winfrey, Beyonce Knowles found her passion at a very early age. Since then, she has made her work revolve around that passion – music and performing. While she went for auditions, she met a future music partner, Kelly Rowland, with whom she would form a music group called Destiny's Child formerly Girls Tyme. Although the challenges that came with pursuing her passion eventually broke up her family, Beyonce continued. As she started to make progress, her family was back together again. Eventually, she signed a contract with Sony Music, along with her group and it has been an upward trajectory for Beyonce since then. By 2017, Forbes rated her as the richest woman in music with a net worth of 350 million dollars, overtaking Britney Spears.

These two women have built laudable careers from following their passion. While following your passion does not make the work any easier, it makes you more welcoming of the challenges that might come your way. One thing you will find out is that once you make your passion your work, it comes with an entirely new demand. Thus, although you might love singing, when it becomes your work, then you have to sing songs not just for fun, but be good enough to return revenue to you and the people who manage you. You have to be at the top of your game as often as possible.

Your passion is something that prompts you to give your all. But, before deciding to make your passion your work, ask these three questions,
1.      Why am I passionate about this?
2.      What are my ambitions in life?
3.      What will people pay for?

When you choose to make your passion your work, you must ensure that it can help you attain your future financial, social and emotional aspirations. If you do not carefully consider this, you might eventually let go of that passion when you get to an even more difficult point in your life. Remember that it will not always be about you, especially if you also choose to build a family and are fully or partially responsible for some of the people around you. You need to put this in view. Where do you see yourself in the next ten years? Will making your passion your work get you there or will you rather complement your passion with another job? You need to think strategically about your future as you make this decision. Yet, remember to be fearless in going after your passion. There is nothing more painful than a life full of regrets. So do a careful analysis and make the best decision that will ensure you not only have a happy work life, but also a desirable future.

To this end, you have to be careful when making that decision. Another thing you must avoid is mixing up your hobby with your passion.

While sometimes, both are one and the same, your hobby is significantly different from your passion.

## DIFFERENTIATING BETWEEN A HOBBY AND A PROFITABLE PASSION

Going through some of the steps on how to find your passion above will leave you with a list of things you like doing. However, this does not imply that it will be the same list as your hobbies. A common mistake people make is to mix up their passion with their hobbies.

What hobbies and passion have in common is that both may be enjoyable activities. Unlike hobbies, passion requires much more sacrifice. Your passion includes those things you are willing to do even when things are not favourable. It is something you must be willing to suffer for, if there is a need. You can easily forgo your hobbies when you have little chance to engage in them. However, things you are passionate about do not leave you. While it is possible you never have to choose between your passion and other important things in your life, when you do, it is usually a very difficult conversation to have with yourself and other people who are involved.

Come rain, come shine, your passion lives in your heart. The same cannot be said for a hobby which changes as your status, opportunities, location, and interest changes. There is no bad day to pursue your passion. However, hobbies are mostly for good days. Essentially, you usually engage in your hobbies at your leisure time, while your passion is something that fills up your work and perhaps eats into your leisure time. If your passion is not your work, then it is that thing that makes you spend less time with your work. It is what you are willing to sacrifice your convenience, leisure time, money and time doing. It is something you can barely stay away from acting on.

Despite this, it might still be difficult to know what your passion is, while hobbies are quite easy to acknowledge.

### What If my Passion Cannot Generate Income—

One of the feedback I get from people who I share my ideas about passion and career with is that question; what do I do if my passion is not exactly profitable?

It is possible to have a passion that only gives you emotional satisfaction, and has little way of rewarding you financially. Of course, your passion should reward you. I however acknowledge that some of our work may not reward us financially as they do in other ways, for example, emotionally.

We are in a world where value is mostly exchanged for money. Therefore, dedicating all your time to a passion that might not yield financial reward can mean that you are signing up for a less than abundant life. The first question will be, "Are you satisfied with having little finances because you are pursuing your passion?" I envisage that some people have no problem with living a frugal life but most people want to live a life of abundance.

For those who are open to a more financially rewarding career, one of the things people who encounter this situation do is that they get a job that fulfils their financial needs while also allowing them enough freedom to go after their passion. Being able to manage two different commitments can be a lot of work. However, when you are able to connect following your passion with your job and understand that both are pieces of a whole puzzle, it becomes more comprehensible. You find harmony in the two and can acknowledge that you are unable to do one without the other. Perhaps, things might change and the world will create a market for your passion. But until then, you need to fulfil your emotional and financial needs, and this is one simple way to achieve it. For example, one of my colleagues loves to travel. While she was unable to secure a job that allowed her travel as often as she wanted, she got a well-paying job that could comfortably finance her vacations.

Thus for someone like Florence who may be unable to leave her job, there are options. After she might have gone through the process of identifying her passion, she can find one way or another to pursue that passion until she finds the perfect opportunity to maximize it.

Another way to find out how you can maximize your passion is to sit with a career counsellor who might understand how to build a career out of your passion.

Perhaps, the only reason you think your passion might not have any potential to provide consistent income is because you do not know anyone with similar passion who is making money from it. Working with a counsellor can help you uncover ways to turn your passion into your work.

Finally, you may also spend some time alone trying to design a way for you to make a business out of our passion. Through critical and creative thinking and some understanding of how businesses work, it is possible you attain a breakthrough in successfully designing a model that enables you make consistent and reliable income from your passion.

Building on a passion that renders you unable to sustain yourself or your aspirations can have a negative impact on you. Thus, it is important to always ensure that you are not a slave to your passion. Your passion should be modelled to make you happy. Happiness comes from both enjoying what you do, and knowing that you will always be fine doing it. When fear begins to creep into your activities, it becomes less enjoyable. That is why it is critical to channel your passion profitably, or do profitable work to support your passion. In the end, sustainability is essential. As we discussed earlier in Chapter 1, man's most important needs which sit at the bottom of the Maslow's Hierarchy of Needs must be served. Creating a fulfilling and rewarding career around your passion will ensure that you continue to enjoy that passion.

The key to unlocking your passion is to not abandon it. Remember, the mind is a powerful thing. When properly explored, the mind can think up amazing ways to accomplish things that we never thought possible. Notwithstanding, if you are unable to crack a business out of your passion, you can explore the other alternatives highlighted, like using your job to fuel your passion.

So far, we have been able to identify what it takes to start on the journey to build a fulfilling and rewarding career, the different career paths and how you may find and channel your career into your passion. In the next chapter, I look at how you may address your career when things are already going wrong. I believe this calls for a different approach as you are now under even more pressure to make sense of your career.

SECTION THREE

# Taking Action - Building the Career You Desire

CHAPTER FOUR

# CAREER PLANNING: CHOOSING OR CHANGING A CAREER

*"Believe in yourself. You are braver than you more talented than you know, and capable of more than you imagine."*

**-Roy T. Bennett**

It is easy to get lost in both the sameness and the vicissitudes of your work life. In attending seemingly unending meetings, signing attendances, engaging in or avoiding corporate politics, working hard to meet targets and fighting to keep your job, you can lose track of time and be left unable to properly channel your career into what you want. In the midst of these activities, building a career that provides you great personal reward and satisfaction remains important.

Building a conscious career is a choice; it is not something you just stumble on. That choice starts from taking deliberate steps to plan and act on the way you want your career to evolve. It is about you taking steps to build actionable plans on your vision for your career lifespan.

The process of designing your career in a way you want it to unfold is referred to as Career Planning. There are two ways you may look at this; you may plan forward or plan backward. Planning forward means identifying where you are now, and planning towards the future. Planning backward means looking at where you want to be in a definite number of years, say 20 years, and walking backwards to your current position with an action plan on what you need to do to get to that point.

In previous chapters, I discussed how to find your passion and channel it into your career. I have been careful not to suggest what kind of career you should pursue. I believe the more important thing is letting you understand the different paths you can channel your career and how you can choose what is best for you. If so far, you have been able to find your passion or are closer to doing so, then you have made remarkable progress.

In addition, we discussed how to merge your passion with your career. This is the hallmark of a conscious career; doing what you love and doing it in the best possible way – a way that rewards you financially and emotionally.

This chapter is about taking the next step after you have identified what you like to do and how you like to do it.

After you have decided whether you are in the right career or not, what truly matters are the steps you take towards achieving your career goals.

The following are the next important steps to take that will move you closer to the peak of your career.

**BELIEVE IN YOURSELF**

Whether you think you can, or whether you think you can't, you're right – Henry Ford

More than genius, it takes courage to make things happen, whether for you or for the world. The first place to start is to know and acknowledge that you are capable of achieving your goals; of being more than you currently are. If you do not think you have the capacity to move up the career ladder, you will not. Your mindset is very important. Is your mind set up for growth or is it set up starkly with limitations? Do you believe you can grow 10 times your current capacity? Do you think you have what it takes to move forward? Do you believe in yourself enough to trust yourself with your career growth?

We will discuss several steps in this book that will guide you to take the right steps towards your career growth. However, I cannot promise it will work for people who do not believe it can work for them. A lack of belief in yourself or in a process, no matter how easy or straightforward, will only limit your chances of being successful. A key secret to success is self-belief and I cannot emphasize this enough. Having met tons of employees and founders in my career, I have found that one of the greatest limitations to building a financially rewarding and fulfilling career is one's inability to envision a better future for self. It stems from the fact that as much as people want a better life, several think it is beyond them. Perhaps they think it is too late to make attempts at taking giant steps or they think the environment will not accommodate their progress. Some people have this mental model that informs their limited thinking and pushes them to believe that making progress in their career is only possible through unscrupulous means or luck. If you are unable to imagine a better world for yourself, then taking actions on ideas from this book will be quite difficult to do. But, if you are currently at this stage, and you believe you can experience change in your mindset, then that is a good starting point.

When you start believing in yourself, great things happen. You are more confident about taking charge of your life, and you are in a better position to build a conscious career. In the words of one of the famous painters of Western Art, Vincent van Gogh;

"If you hear a voice within you say 'you cannot paint,' then by all means paint, and that voice will be silenced."

In order to overcome your fears, you only need to start believing in your ability to make things happen. Caging yourself within limitations framed by your own mind is undermining your potentials. You have to break loose from them and set your mind free. You have to hold yourself to a higher standard and believe you can experience the future you seek. You have to demand more from yourself. Remember, if you believe you can, then you can. And if your belief is that you can't, then you can't. One of the major differences between successful people and unsuccessful people is that the former believe they can make things happen. We all usually have to deal with uncertainties, fears, constraints and failure. However, when you believe you can reach your goals regardless of what happens, you set yourself on the path to success.

A hack to help kick start your self-belief is to talk to people who love you and believe in you. When you engage in meaningful conversations with these people who are likely to be your friends or relatives, tell them about the challenge you currently have. In more ways than one, they can remind you of the great qualities you possess, especially by relating past experiences where you did remarkably well. Another hack is, you may sit down and list some of your past accomplishments, especially the ones you were excited about achieving. When you make this list, try to recollect how you accomplished them and how you felt when you did.

Although the work is very demanding and requires a lot of strategic thinking, especially to keep it going due to limited resources, I am excited about the chance to do great work that highly impacts the lives of others. However, I am not enjoying recurring financial stability which I believe should be part of it. This is partly because I have been unable to crack how to build a sustainable social enterprise. My income is irregular and sometimes, I go a few months without generating any income for myself. This is usually worrisome.

## SETTING OBJECTIVES
"If you do not know where you are going, every road will get you nowhere."- **Henry A Kissinger**

If you have given a thought to how you want your career to unfold, this is the point where you start. After coming to a decision on what your career status is, this is the point where you determine where you want to be by the end of your career. The purpose is to help you plot a path that gets you to your career goals.

When setting objectives, you must keep them SMART. This means your objectives must be Specific, Measurable, Achievable, Realistic and Timely. You must be specific with your goals, while keeping it simple. Setting objectives you are unable to measure is a recipe for disaster. You must be able to tell how far you have come in achieving that objective and how far you need to go. Your objectives must also be achievable and realistic. While you may not already have a plan for achieving your objectives, it is important for you to picture your objectives and understand the possibility of achieving them, using present resources. Finally, it is necessary to keep your objectives time-bound.

You should break your objectives into long, medium and short term periods. Ensure that there is a progression from the short term objectives to the long term objectives. This will keep you from breaking off at a point while trying to reach unrealistic targets.

A simple example is:

- Long term goal - I want to be one of the top 20 gynaecologists in my city in 15 years and set up my private practice.
- Medium term goal - I want to be invited to make a presentation of my work and research in at least five global conferences in the next five years.
- Short term goal - I want to rise to become one of the best gynaecologists in my hospital in the next one year.

You may have more than one objective; the important thing is that they follow the SMART rule. Your objective should describe what you intend to do in the near future. Thus, if your choice is to maintain a career in the field you are currently in, then it makes sense to plot your future along that field. However, if you plan to change your career, then your objective has to be in line with that career. For example,

- Long term goal - I currently work as a Doctor but in 15 years, I want to be one of the renowned health and wellness life coaches in Nigeria.
- Medium term goal - In the next four years, I want to set up my private practice as a life coach in Nigeria.
- Medium term goal - In the next two years, I want to master the 11 core competences required to be a life coach and become certified.
- Short term goal - In the next one year, I want to take at least 2 life coaching training programs accredited by the International Coaching Federation (ICF).

This way, you have included what you currently are, what you want to be, and you can already begin to draw out steps on how to get there. Remember to write this down.

**WHAT IS YOUR WHY—**
"The two most important days in your life are the day you are born and the day you find out why." **—Mark Twain.**

While it is possible to choose what you want to be from the top of your hat, especially after you have been exposed to some careers that grabbed your interest, it is important to understand why you are choosing a career. What is your why? Your why is the purpose, cause or belief that inspires you to make certain decisions or follow certain career paths. When you know your why, you can make better choices in your career that will help you attain greater fulfilment in the things you do. You have a clear sense of why what you do matters. Fulfilment is better achieved when you live your life on purpose rather than spontaneously. Spontaneity can be good, but it is important that you're deliberate about building a career that is both fulfilling and financially rewarding.

---

**MEDITATION POINT**

Ask yourself:
- Why does this career matter to me?
- How does this career choice make me feel?
- Is this the only career path that can make me feel that way?
- If the answer is no, what are my other options?

---

When you live your life with a sense of purpose, you begin to live positively and seek out new opportunities. Understanding your why puts you on the path to career success. This reminds me of another favourite quote of mine;

"He who has a why can endure any how." - **Friedrich Nietzsche**

**QUALITY TAKES TIME**

I imagine that you know this subconsciously and probably only wonder if you will be able to put in the time required to hit your targets. In many cases, it takes years of constantly and consistently investing efforts to reach the peak of your career or do something remarkable. Excellence takes a little bit more time than we like to imagine.

This may help you set more realistic goals, but for champions, what it does is to make them willing to commit to putting in the long hours to ensure that their dreams work. People who are deliberate about building a career that is fulfilling and financially rewarding understand that the race to their goals is not a sprint, but a marathon. They understand that to build a successful career, one must be patient and persevere. While quick wins will motivate them to go after the next milestone, they do not forget that reaching their ultimate goal can take more time than they estimate. Yet, they believe that however long it takes, they will reach their ultimate goal.

And this is why you need to understand why you are pursuing a career. When you have a why, you become more prepared mentally and physically to go through the vicissitudes of building a remarkable career.

## ASK FOR HELP

As we discussed earlier, achieving remarkable heights in your career, whether you are sticking to your current field or changing to a new field, will require a lot of input from you. Thus, when you feel stuck or better still, before you get stuck, you should be open to consulting colleagues, friends or any other learned person on what to do next.

One of the first steps in improving your knowledge base regarding your career is to go online and try to learn more about that particular career or the career you intend to venture into. Reading provides you with insights from people who have had to take similar decisions as you want to take, and helps you to know more about your field than you currently do. Read books, read articles and ask questions where you need clarification.

You can ask a senior colleague at work who may have more experience than you do or ask colleagues who may have taken similar decisions in the past. A popular Yoruba proverb goes thus, "A person who asks for directions does not get lost."

Don't get lost.

## CHANGING TIMES
"I can't change the direction of the wind, but I can adjust my sails to always reach my destination." **Jimmy Dean**

Whether you're choosing your career or changing it, you should acknowledge that the world is constantly changing and you must prepare for that change. Your goals may remain, especially when they are not tied to a target that is too specific. Goals must revolve around your why, but your methods must revolve around the current state of the world. Your methods must remain flexible and realistic so that in any circumstance, you can keep going.

As the world continues to move forward, it is quite possible that some of the jobs we have today will become simple tasks for machines. This essentially eliminates all careers built around those jobs; except, of course, for those who can anticipate and adapt to change. Less than 50 years ago, clerks were a main feature in any administrative block. In this present time, most people can now do without clerks, especially at emerging companies. This is because personal computers have taken over most of the roles that a typical clerk used to do. Similar to this, people are now using accounting softwares to keep their books, effectively eliminating the need for a full time accountant. We may not be able to determine the future of work, but we can determine how we adjust our sails to its winds, so we are not thrown overboard.

## INTRINSIC AND EXTRINSIC MOTIVATION

"What lies behind us and what lies before us are tiny matters compared to what lies within us." **– Ralph Waldo Emerson**

Motivation is an important fuel to reaching the peak of your career, and where your motivation comes from is critical to sustaining it. Psychologists classify motivation into two; intrinsic motivation and extrinsic motivation. Intrinsic motivation is a natural desire to master and pursue a cause. The reasons for that desire are innate. Others may understand it as self-motivation. Self-motivation is the ability to do what needs to be done, without influence from other people or situations.

Extrinsic motivation is the desire to pursue a cause for reasons outside the individual. Such reasons include but are not limited to societal approval, tangible and intangible rewards. When you are motivated intrinsically, you do things because they are naturally satisfying to you. It means whether or not external factors change, you will still find it within yourself to pursue that cause or do that thing.

On the other hand, extrinsic motivation is heavily dependent on the external environment. This includes an environment that is conducive, financial rewards, bonuses, praise and recognition, etc. It may also be fear or the desire to avoid punishment. People are generally more creative when motivation is internal. While both motivation classes play major roles in driving us towards our goals, it is important that for something as critical and personal as a career, especially one built on your passion, you should be intrinsically motivated. Indeed, for a conscious career, you need to be driven internally more than anything else. Your passion and purpose must come from within. Famous American football coach, Homer Rice, underlines the importance of self-motivation;

"You can motivate by fear, and you can motivate by reward. But both those methods are only temporary. The only lasting thing is self-motivation."

## PREPARE FINANCIALLY

As you head on to make yourself better at your career, I must highlight that you will need to invest more in yourself. Trying to improve your career based on only your personal experience is slow and tedious. Thus, you may need to take some courses, buy some books or attend trainings. All these come at a cost.

If you are looking to change your career, you should seek the financial cost of your intention.
Knowing that you may be unemployed for some time means that you should save enough money to give you the ability to sustain yourself during the time between jobs and create a financial management plan to live successfully on your budget during this period of transition.

71

The table below provides a simple guide and summary to this chapter. I have used the example of a gynaecologist who wants to be one of the best in the country. Notice that we started with the long term goal and then drilled it down to the short term goal. This is because in our approach, it is necessary for your short term goals to be milestones that enable you move closer to your long term goals. Thus, as you start this, you should state your long term goal and then create the objectives you have to meet to get there. Remember that nothing is set in stone. You are at liberty to make changes due to new realities. What matters ultimately is that you keep your eyes on your eventual goal.

GOAL: To be one of the most renowned gynaecologists in Nigeria in 15 years.

| OBJECTIVE | PERIOD | WHY | WHAT I NEED TO DO | WHAT I CURRENTLY HAVE | WHAT I NEED TO GET | ESTIMATED FINANCIAL IMPLICATION |
|---|---|---|---|---|---|---|
| LONG TERM | | | | | | |
| Set up private practice. | 5 years. | To widen my practice and enhance my influence. | Build a reservoir of potential clients from existing clients.<br><br>Start saving for real estate and medical equipment.<br><br>Gain recognition in the industry as a reputable gynaecologist.<br><br>Specialize in a field and get certifications. | 2 years' experience as a gynaecologist.<br><br>A growing list of potential clients. | Additional qualifications.<br><br>Get published in medical journals.<br><br>Public presentation of academic papers at global conferences.<br><br>Funds to start private practice. | 25 million Naira. |

| MEDIUM TERM | | | | | | |
|---|---|---|---|---|---|---|
| Present my academic research in 5 conferences. | 3 years. | To reach a larger audience with my knowledge and expertise. | Publish my paper in five different widely read journals. Send my application to request audience to at least 10 conferences. Prepare financially to travel to these conferences. | My academic research paper. | Access to key journals. More experience in my practice. | 3 million Naira. |

| SHORT TERM | | | | | | |
|---|---|---|---|---|---|---|
| Get additional relevant qualification. | 18 Months | To improve my knowledge about my profession and specialize in a specific industry. | Find a reputable institution offering online options. Apply to the institution. Review current lifestyle to accommodate study. | Personal laptop to use for online study. | Tuition and feeding expenses. | 2 million Naira. |

CHAPTER FIVE

# LEARNING AND
# CONTINUOUS DEVELOPMENT

*"The more that you read, the more you will know.*
*The more you learn, the more places you'll go"*
**– Dr Seuss.**

In the previous chapter, I outlined the process of setting actionable objectives to get the best out of your career. This chapter is about taking the steps to increase your capacity in order to achieve those goals. I will be honest with you; to get yourself to the right capacity that will help you to achieve all your goals, you must engage in continuous learning and self-development in line with your career. There is just no way to escape this. If you close the door to conscious continuous learning, you close the door to a conscious prosperous career. It is as simple as that.

Several people put an end to their learning once they get a job. If you probe, their last formal education experience was probably prior to their graduation from tertiary institution. Since then, it has been work, work and more work. Engaging in work without plans for learning is the prime recipe for stagnancy or a sluggish career growth. Why grow arithmetically, when you can grow exponentially? And that is what continuous learning does; it leads to exponential growth in your career. Let us start by admitting that you are a work in progress, we all are actually. The moment you begin to feel you are the finished product, please retire as there is no need to keep going. A good analogy of an average professional can be described using a flower plant. Every person is a flower plant. Acquiring new knowledge is what you use to replenish the plant. If you do not water this plant, it will begin to wither and eventually die. You remain the same when you do not improve yourself, and after a while, you start to fall behind. This can lead to stagnancy as well as degeneration. The reason is not far-fetched; the world is constantly moving, constantly changing, and those who do not advance with it, get left behind.

Even beyond using it to fuel your career growth, there are many more reasons to engage in continuous learning. Here are some of them:

- To keep up with trends in your career
The way we do work continues to experience great changes. In the past decade, the requirement to fill different roles in different industries has dramatically changed. First, if you compare how we search for work between the last decade and now, you can surmise that things are different.

You probably did not require a LinkedIn account and there was no Jobberman to connect you with jobs. This means that if you do not follow the trend and learn to make yourself available on these platforms, you might miss many opportunities that would have elevated you in your career much faster.

Being computer literate is now an important skill, even for school teachers. During my time with a technology company, I worked on a project that equipped schools with a smart learning solution, which meant students and teachers had a personal handheld device and/or computer with which they shared notes, received and submitted assignments and sometimes wrote exams with. If as a teacher you had not learnt to be proficient with using computers with modern day software, thinking it has little to do with how you taught in class, you will appear incompetent no matter how good you are with your 'teaching'. Thus, continuous learning keeps us abreast of the trends in our career and helps us to move forward, ensuring we remain relevant in our careers.

### - The more you learn, the more you earn
I believe many people know this already. We have numerous people who pursue a master's degree so that they can qualify for new positions within or outside their organizations. Take the Nigerian military for example; graduates are more likely to reach the peak of their military careers than non-graduates. The success of an organization is highly dependent on the people behind it. These people work every day to improve the business and deliver on the organization's promise. Knowledgeable managers understand that they need good talent to grow their companies; which is why companies generally pay people who have more expertise and understand their market better a lot higher than those who do not. Continuous learning positions you for higher income.

### - Retain your employment
When companies are going through a change phase or are in a difficult period, they usually let off employees from their payroll. Many times, this does not include employees the company believes contribute great value to them and who remain relevant for the phase they are going through.

During such times, companies are looking to cut down cost but still remain operational, while speeding up their return to stability. They require the best of their talents without incurring the extra cost of recruitment. If you have positioned yourself to be better at your work, you are more likely to remain on the ship while it steadies.

When a company is going through this phase, which sometimes is caused by a change in technology, strategy or policy, you will still retain your job while the company lets others go. This is because you have kept yourself abreast of the changes going on in your industry. You have also prepared yourself adequately for the possibility of your company adopting some of these new changes. One thing you should utilize to your advantage is the reality that it actually costs a company more to get new staff than to retain old ones. Thus, when companies go out of their way to recruit new talent, it is because certain roles cannot be filled by their current staff.

## - Not easily replaced
If you are not getting better, you will be replaced. Whether by alternative technology, or by a better professional, it is going to happen. Continuous learning makes you invaluable. You become a resource that is too good to lose. It becomes even better when you are so good that you are able to train some of your colleagues, as that automatically raises your profile. Companies are happier when they have the best talents. Throwing yourself into this mix of best talents should be your goal. If your company is happy to have you work for them, you hold a better bargaining power over work decisions and compensation.

## - Building networks
When you go all out to learn, you find yourself in a network of people who are also forward thinking. I met quite a number of influential people while pursuing my master's degree in International Relations and Strategic Studies, some of whom I might not have come across as easily outside that circle. These people would eventually become invaluable contacts whose relationships have been instrumental to my career growth.

More importantly, due to the fact that you are likely to have similar interests with those in your learning group, you can share resources to facilitate one another's progress.

**- Improve productivity by developing your skills and abilities**
Another key reason you should engage in learning after you may have secured a job is to become more proficient at your work. There is no point spending several hours doing work you can accomplish within a shorter time if you understood it better. While some companies go through the pains of training their employees periodically, you should not wait till that point before you seek to become better. Attaining improved productivity improves the quality of work you deliver and reduces the amount of time you would have spent doing it. Improve your ability to align your career for impact by learning efficient ways to deliver your impact.

It is easy to build a career that benefits only you. Or maybe it is not that easy. Regardless, if your goal is to build a career that has high positive impact on you and the people around you, then it is important to learn how. Becoming a force for good requires strategic thinking, else you might believe you are helping people but they do not feel your impact. Continuous learning helps you understand people and processes better, so that you can make better decisions about your career.

## THE DIFFERENT TYPES OF CAREER LEARNING

Brian Tracy is one of the most respected and recognized life coaches in
the world. He is the author of over 60 books on sales, management,
business success and personal development. One of his widely read
publications is the 'Psychology of Achievement', a personal
development book that became a world bestseller. In this book, Tracy
classified learning into three categories:

### Maintenance Learning

Maintenance learning is gaining knowledge that keeps you abreast in
your field, and involves following new information about your field.
This process is absolutely essential as it ensures that while you work
arduously to deliver on key goals for your work, you remain in the loop
on the trends that occur in your field. Maintenance learning includes
following both industry and general news that can help you keep up
with the happenings in your career and ensure you are not left behind.
Just like you take a car to the mechanic to do maintenance checks,
maintenance learning makes sure you are at the right place in your
career.

79

With maintenance learning, you must be consistent in your reception of new information.

### Growth Learning
This type of learning helps you improve your skills and knowledge. It is about pursuing learning that provides you with new knowledge and abilities that you did not possess beforehand. When you continuously learn for growth, you improve your capability, expand your mind, identify new horizons and enhance your understanding of your field.

Growth learning can be achieved by reading books, online journals, listening to podcasts, taking a course or attending trainings on innovations in products and best practices in your industry. It advances you to a higher stage in your career and gives you the ability to take on bigger challenges.

### Shock Learning
This type of learning helps you to refine your thinking. Alvin Toffler, a philosopher, was once quoted to have said,

"The illiterate of the 21st century will not be those who cannot read and write, but those who cannot learn, unlearn, and relearn."

At different times of gathering knowledge, it is possible that some of the knowledge we might have acquired before then are no longer valid. What shock learning does is to provide an alternative understanding of what we thought we knew, usually contradicting our previous understanding of it. While some people might be rebellious in accepting such new information, people who become successful are keen to examine the new knowledge, understand it and seek out any opportunity it presents.

When things happen that are not consistent with your expectations, rather than fight it, seek to understand it. You must not be afraid of change. You must remain flexible with knowledge, learn to adapt quickly and seek to use new knowledge as you come into it, to advance your career. Remember that the goal is not to be a knowledge bank, but to acquire useful knowledge that can get you to the peak of your career.

An important philosophy we discussed in the previous chapter was Kaizen. The idea behind continuous improvement is an important one for everyone to adopt. Your ability to go from zero to one and on and on till you get to hundred will help you get the best out of your career. Rather than focus on the things you do not know, list out some of the things you want to learn and focus on achieving them one step after the other. The popular saying, Rome was not built in a day, applies to your career development. You cannot go from being a newbie to a veteran in a single jump. However, as a newbie, you can begin to take steps towards becoming a veteran at any stage of your career. Your goal is to become better to a point that no one can ignore you, not to mention the fact that continuous learning sets you apart from the rest of the pack.

## WHAT ROUTES CAN YOU EMPLOY TO IMPROVE YOUR KNOWLEDGE AND SKILL

### Formal education
Despite the varieties of places where you can engage in learning, formal institutions still represent the foremost way of acquiring industry related knowledge, although this is mostly true for countries where the curriculums are up to date with modern demands. Formal education provides structures and facilities that help you learn. More importantly, it puts you in a network of people with shared interest. I was quite excited to be at the University of Reading for my postgraduate course in Communication for Innovation and Development. It exposed me to a network of people from all over the world, some of whom I am still in touch with to this day. The disadvantage to formal education is that it can be too structured sometimes and expensive. Most times, you also have to take a break from your work to attend classes.

### Online courses
The rise of technology in the 21st century presented a new dimension to learning. Open Online Courses have become a big deal and provide a new way to stay connected to the best learning experiences at your convenience.

This means that all you have to do to acquire formal and informal learning from some of the best tutors in the world is a computer, internet access and maybe some money. While the experience is not as intimate as a 'real' classroom, Massive Open Online Courses (MOOCs) are similarly efficient in dispersing learning and sharing academic experiences and knowledge. Some online platforms that offer useful courses include Coursera, Udemy, Udacity, Alison and so on. These platforms also allow you build on your soft skills. Some courses on these platforms are free while you will be required to pay for others.

## Trainings and Conferences

Attending trainings can be another way to acquire knowledge. Not all trainings are useful, hence you should be able to identify the ones that are good for you and will move you closer to your career goals. Since there is no verification system to help you know which trainings will be beneficial, you should try to do some research about the trainings you wish to attend. What are other people saying about them and their experience with them? What previous events have they done and how did they turn out? Do they have a good presence and track record in the industry? The type of facilitators they have lined up for the training can also give you an idea of what to expect. Time is of essence to a person building a conscious career and it should not be spent attending trainings that add nothing to you.

## Personal Learning

"Formal education will make you a living; self-education will make you a fortune." - **Jim Rohn**

I believe many people undermine their ability to sit and use materials to improve their knowledge and skill. Usually, it is people who have no choice that teach themselves new skills. Perhaps, that is why many people take it for granted, because they believe they can access good teachers and classrooms anytime they want. I will join other renowned persons to say Self Education is one of the best forms of education you can avail yourself.

I believe formal education has its place, but if a person cannot cultivate the discipline and habit for self-education, her progress will be sluggish. You cannot apply to a university every time to acquire new knowledge you deem important. In fact, if you do not cultivate the habit of self-education, your chance of reaching the peak of your career is very limited.

One story that inspires me is that of William Kamkwamba, the Malawian teenager who built a windmill using scraps from the dump yard. After dropping out of school due to his parents' inability to keep up with the fees, Kamkwamba resorted to the local library where he picked interest in a book titled 'Using Energy'. By applying the knowledge in this book, William built a windmill at the age of 14 which supplied power to his house that sufficiently lighted up four bulbs and powered two radios. William would eventually speak at TED to a global audience about his initiative. He then went on to receive a scholarship to the African Leadership Academy and in 2014, he graduated from Dartmouth College, in Hanover, New Hampshire. His ability to educate himself put his career on an exciting and extraordinary trajectory that his peers may never get to attain.

## LEARNING BY DOING

"Tell me and I forget. Teach me and I remember. Involve me and I learn." - Benjamin Franklin
While you may go wild after knowledge, ensure that you do not become a knowledge dump; that is, the lady who knows everything but has not done anything.

## LET YOUR LEARNING BE PURPOSEFUL

Perhaps we have heard throughout our lives that we should acquire as much knowledge as possible. Thus, we are encouraged to read very wide. While this is important, you must be able to coordinate the knowledge you acquire with a goal. The way graphic artists use Photoshop, for example, is not the same way user interface designers use it. Even though the two have learnt how to use the design software, they learnt it to achieve different purposes.

Knowledge should be a tool you use to advance your career or attain a goal. When you see it this way, you will begin to acquire knowledge differently. You will be more purposeful in your pursuit of knowledge.

That is why we discussed setting your objectives before setting out to acquire more knowledge. This is to ensure that the knowledge you set out to acquire aligns with the goals you plan to achieve. You cannot read all the books in the world. You probably cannot even read all the books published in a single year. With this limitless repository of knowledge and the limited time you have to read, prioritization becomes key. Therefore, with the sea of information, it is necessary to sift out the clutter and go after knowledge that is useful to you. Building a conscious career is about understanding how to use different tools to deliberately move you towards the peak of your career.

## BUILD YOUR SOFT SKILLS
Aside from working to become better at your profession, you should not forget to acquire some of these skills as well:

### Time management
I cannot overemphasise the obvious fact that we all have limited time to be everything we want to be. Is that time enough? Absolutely. People have done amazing things within 24 hours a day and some people reach great heights within a short time and at a young age. While we may not develop at the same pace, it is necessary to learn how to use our time more effectively. If you cannot do this and you find yourself wasting time often, you should take a course or use tools that can help you keep to time. Some tools you can use include To Do, Toggl, Todoist, Google Calendar, to mention a few.

### Task management
Being able to manage your task such that you fulfil them in time and properly is key to your progress. Thus, learning how to manage your tasks, whether singly or with teams, is a necessity. For more complex tasks, you may need to specifically learn project management, but you would not need to do so for simple daily tasks. Instead, you can use applications such as Asana, Trello, Wunderlist and so on.

## Leadership and Conflict Resolution

When you work with people, you do need to be able to display leadership skills and resolve conflicts that may come up at work. You do not have to be in a leadership position to show leadership initiative. When you assume that role in any situation through your actions, you are taking charge of your career and subsequently your life. A course in emotional intelligence will of great help.

## Presentation skills

I singled this out because I have noticed that many people have awesome ideas but cannot effectively share them, especially when they get in front of the right audience. Since it is unlikely that most of us can achieve the extraordinary without the help of others, it is necessary for you to be able to sell your ideas or vision to other people in a way that will make them keen to join your cause. Sometimes, it is not even this deep; you might just want to tell people about your work and what you have achieved so far, and you start to flounder. Work at improving your presentation skills. Lucky for you, there are a number of free resources, including videos, to help you do that.

## Work Applications

It is the 21st century, and you should learn how to use basic applications that are instrumental to your work. Applications such as word processors like Word and Google Docs, Excel and Google Sheets, PowerPoint and Google Slides are some of the easy to use software which are important to today's world of work. Also learn to use social media constructively.

Other soft skills you should look to develop are communication and interpersonal skills, cognitive and critical thinking, problem solving, emotional intelligence. You may also find out which ones are important to your industry and learn them.

Your learning should never stop. You can learn from colleagues as much as you learn from formal classes and books.

Be open to taking in new information. However, know that as you become more open to new information, you also open yourself to non-useful information, so you must learn to sift through the noise.

CHAPTER SIX

# WHAT TO DO WHEN THINGS ARE NOT WORKING OUT

*"Growth is painful. Change is painful. But, nothing is as painful as staying stuck where you do not belong."*
- **N. R. Narayana Murthy**

Kate's biggest worry as she continued to plough her efforts in line with her passion was that she was beginning to feel exhausted. At different times, she had begun to feel disengaged and unproductive. She had taken the advice to follow her passion because people who follow their passion enjoy every day of work, but now, she was beginning to have second thoughts about the said work. Could she have chosen the wrong passion? Is it normal to tire out while doing the thing you believe you enjoy the most?

The questions Florence asked herself at work disturbed her. She had continued to wonder whether to hold onto or quit her job. Getting out of the workforce and joining the hordes of unemployed people did not seem like something she looked forward to doing. Notwithstanding, she was certain that she was no longer challenged at work and continued to feel a gap between what she was doing and what she thought she was capable of doing. It is the reason she continued to question herself about her passion. Perhaps, if she was doing work she was passionate about, she will be driven to do great work.

Kate and Florence were at a point where several people find themselves at different points in their career. For some people, they have been putting in a lot of effort in their work and have been unable to find fulfilment. Others are unable to manage the volume of work that their job demands especially since there is a disconnection between what they do and where their passion lies.

I have come across a lot of people who suddenly feel they don't fit where they currently are. They are either consciously seeking a way out of their current job or hoping that the dynamics change. Many of us would have worked at places not quite as comfortable as you envisage your workplace to be. Some people are unlucky to work at places where they are unable to grow, do not have fun working and are still paid below the minimum wage. Several factors can cause us to feel like our career is not going in the right direction. Aside from passion, these are some of the things that can make an employee feel like things are not working properly.

## 1. There is no growth

This is when you cannot see an improvement in your career as a result of the work you do. For something as important as a career, we want to continue to move up a ladder that leads us to a new experience, rather than falling down a pit or feeling stuck at a particular point for several years.

Growth can come in two ways; growth inspired by you or growth inspired by your profession. For employees, they need to be able to see that in a number of years moving forward, they would have attained new heights within that job. And their employer must facilitate that growth. While for others, they want to see a clear path and possibility of progression in the field they have chosen to work. When people feel stuck in their work, they automatically get frustrated. Sometimes, they are actually not stuck. They are just unable to clearly see progression in their work, especially when compared with other people's work.

Let me paint a picture for you. A person who plants pineapple may feel stuck for a long period, especially when that person can see the sprouts of the maize plant her colleague planted at the same time she planted hers. While pineapple may take two years to grow fully, a maize plant only takes five months. Using that yardstick, such comparison becomes futile. Therefore, when we do not have the right tools to measure our peculiar progressions, we may feel like things are not going our way. To mitigate this, you should understand how to measure your growth at a job. That way, you can take charge of your career and understand the right things to work on to reach your peak.

Growth is usually measured against goals. When you do not clearly define your goals, you are unable to take action towards achieving them. Therefore, if you really want to understand whether you are growing or not, start by setting some goals. One goal can be to improve your network in that field, another might be to rise in ranks, while yet another might relate to your financial goals. When you have set these goals, you can have an informed understanding of whether your organization limits your growth or not.

It is not only your employer than can limit your growth; it may be any authority with power enough to limit your progress within that profession even if that profession clearly allows growth. Such authorities may include the government, regulatory agencies, or a monopoly. The first thing to do in this case is to check if you can negotiate with such authorities to enable you to move forward. For example, you may sit with your employer, discuss your potential for growth within that organization and learn what ways the organization is set up to ensure that growth. It is possible what you think is required for you to move forward is not part of the organization's criteria for promotion. When you make inquiries like that, you are empowered to take charge of your growth within that organization. Things suddenly look clearer and more achievable, or at least better than they were.

If you find that your organization cannot accommodate or prevents the kind of growth you seek in your profession, then it is better to seek a new job where you can improve your capacity. You can make an early switch or you may gradually prepare yourself for that time when you need to move to the next stage, which your current organization does not allow for. For people who are restrained by a government authority, an alternative might be to find a new base where the government is friendlier to your dreams. This transition might require saving up. If you have the capacity to influence the authorities to review regulations in your favour, then you should try that before seeking to change location. Taking charge of your career requires you to deliberately consider options which might lead you to the peak of it. You should not confine yourself to your current situations but constantly seek alternatives and plan your transition.

A final alternative is to exit the profession entirely or if you can, change the dynamics of that job. There are certain roles you eventually recognize do not lead to the ends you desire for yourself. Therefore, growth in such professions does not translate into growth for you. In this case, you feel stuck even though by all indications, you are advancing in your career Although Florence was making remarkable progress in her job and was an enviable example for her colleagues and her friend Kate, she continued to feel like she had a lot of things not going well for her, except of course, the continuous increment in her remuneration which positively impacted her financial status. In this case, Florence could attempt to change the dynamics of her job to include roles that accommodate her desires if the organization permits. Or she could find a job that properly aligns with her desires, such that growth in her career will also mean growth for her.

## 2. There is no fun

More often than not, when your job does not excite you, you begin to feel disengaged. You do not look forward to going to work. When the place where you spend an inordinate amount of your time does not put you in the right mood, then it is normal for you to think things are not going well with your career.

I assume many people do not want to stay in a place that constantly depresses them. While it is possible for your job to be quite monotonous and may require dedicated long hours of work and focus, it is most likely that you will not mind some entertainment to make it more enjoyable. If you are in a job that does not excite you, you may discuss new ideas with your employer to make your work more exciting. Employers are increasingly entertaining fresh ideas on how to make their workplaces more fun. Some have introduced monthly staff hangouts, retreats or periodic getaways when certain milestones are reached (especially for result-driven organizations). There are different ways you may seek to introduce some excitement to your work. However, you must ensure such fun activities do not interfere with your productivity. Instead, such activities should motivate you and colleagues to do better work. Employee Volunteering has proven to be one of the more fulfilling ways to achieving this.

## 3. Poor Remuneration

This is easily one of the biggest reasons people get disillusioned with their career. When you feel you are not properly compensated for your work, you end up mentally exhausted even if you have done very little work. Therefore, whether you are working for an employer or on your own, you should ensure you are satisfied with the immediate and future compensations attached to that work.

Some people may agree to take lower wages at the beginning in hopes that such wages will be raised in the near future. When this does not happen, they start looking for alternatives to bail them from the distress they feel. Hence, when taking up a new job or building a career, you want to pursue one that adequately compensates you, excites you, and offers you progression.

---

**MEDITATION POINT**

These are important questions that can help examine your current job:

- Does my job accommodate the kind of growth that I envisage for myself?
- Will my job continue to be exciting in the way I require it to be as I journey along?
- Does my job compensate me enough to support my life goals?
- What do I need to do if I wish to align my career with my aspirations?

---

## WHAT TO DO WHEN YOU ARE BURNING OUT

While I have talked about all the exciting things passion can breed and how it allows you to put in your best, let me mention that you may also burn out pursuing your passion. During this time, you are exhausted and even wonder if you were correct about where your passion lies.

Burnout is a state of mental and physical exhaustion. If you consistently burn out, you will continue to fall short of your goals and eventually feel like you are not moving forward with your career. Therefore, taking charge of your career requires that you identify potential drawbacks and learn to avoid them, so you can reach your career goals much faster and more efficiently. While building my career, I tried as much as possible to avoid constantly burning out. I acknowledge that there are periods when you are simply unable to prevent such burnout. The important thing, though, is to ensure that it does not become your tradition.

**Here are a few tips you should consider to avoid exhaustion at work.**

### Be Excited About Your Job

Having a more positive attitude to work can help you to overcome burnout. Make a decision not to allow the state of your job to affect your mood. Of course, this requires a huge effort for jobs that would normally depress you. The story of Viktor Frankl continues to inspire me. Victor was one of those in the concentration camps during the Second World War. The kind of atrocities committed by soldiers against those in detention was enough to traumatize any human for the duration of a lifetime. But not Viktor. He decided to shield his inner joy from that experience. While Viktor still had to endure atrocities suffered by others in the concentration camp, he chose to stay positive and soon began to exude that positivity.

"Everything can be taken from a man but one thing: the last of the human freedoms—to choose one's attitude in any given set of circumstances, to choose one's own way." - Viktor Frankl

Thus, while we may find that our jobs are tedious and exhausting, we can attempt to change how they make us feel until we can change the situation to a more favourable one.

### Learn More About the Value Your Company is creating

One important way to reduce the chance of burnout in your work is to understand the value your company creates. This way, you find more meaning in what you do. When you do so, it will raise your desire to go the extra mile to make things happen without feeling immediately exhausted. When you can easily find a connection between your job and the value it creates for other people, you are suddenly willing to give more without feeling lethargic.

I remember a young lady I met sometime, her name is Adeola. Adeola worked as a food vendor in an industrial area. At the early stage of her career, she was easily exhausted by her work, not only because it was exacting, but because she could not see the value she was creating asides providing food for hungry workers.

Then one day, when she could not be at work, one of those workers visited her, and her revelation changed the way Adeola viewed her work going forward. The lady told her about her profession as a pharmacist at a pharmaceutical company. She mentioned that because she could rely on Adeola's food every day while doing her job, she was able to pay better attention to her work; enough to discover new and affordable drugs that could potentially mitigate the effect of diabetes.

Discovering that she was contributing to the progress of healthcare and potentially saving millions of lives indirectly changed the way Adeola viewed her job. Her attitude changed and she was more mentally prepared to take on the demands of the job. The kind of conversations she had with people who ate at her place changed too. She became more interested in their work and ways through which she could add more value to them while increasing her social impact. She even expanded her business offering to delivering food to their desks.

**Review your tasks with the supervisor/manager**
If you are your own boss, review your work to accommodate your current capabilities. If you are an employee, sit with your employer to take a second look at the tasks you currently handle.

"Women, in particular, need to keep an eye on their physical and mental health, because if we're scurrying to and from appointments and errands, we don't have a lot of time to take care of ourselves. We need to do a better job of putting ourselves higher on our own 'to do' list." - **Art Garfunkel**

When you continuously put your health at risk with the volume of tasks you undertake, you risk not being here long enough to reach the peak of your career. Physical and mental exhaustion, more often than not, are caused by stress from work.

Therefore, when you feel that your tasks constantly leave you on the brink of burnout, consider discussing with your manager or reviewing it by yourself, if you have control over the volume.

## Medical Check-ups
An important way to understand what you are capable of handling is to undergo medical check-ups, so you are more certain of the volume of tasks you can take on. When you better understand your health, you can do just enough that is required for you to move fast in your career without jeopardising your health.

## Find More Efficient Ways to do your work
"It's also our collective delusion that overwork and burnout are the price we must pay in order to succeed." — Arianna Huffington

Nobody gets an award for being a workaholic. People are mostly recognized for their performance i.e. how well they got the job done and the result they produced doing the job. Therefore, putting in long hours at work when you can find a way to achieve the same thing within a shorter time and with fewer resources is detrimental to you and your work. Thus, one of the most important reflections of your efficiency at work is being able to identify better and less exhausting ways of doing your work.

Perhaps if you learn that burnouts generally reduce your ability to be at your optimum, it might motivate you to avoid it.

## Take Your Breaks
Go home at the right time. Take your lunch break. Look forward to your leave. Relax during weekends. Enjoy those non-working periods that have been created. Companies are not exactly excited to give you hours off work. However, they know those periods are important to keep you at your best. Therefore, while you will definitely find periods in your career where taking prolonged breaks is detrimental to the speed necessary at that moment, you should not make it your culture not to take time off work. Sometimes, it is okay for something else to be priority for a period, like raising children. Take breaks and during these breaks, engage in enjoyable activities that will help you unwind.

### Sleep

Perhaps, one person that emphasizes the importance of sleep more than most is Arianna Huffington, who even wrote a book about it called, The Sleep Revolution: Transforming Your Life, One Night at a Time. In a bid to do more, many people eat into their sleep time and do not find time to make up for it. Media mogul and billionaire, Arianna Huffington, highlighted through her book that sleep is important to keep us at the top of our game. Sometimes, it is even better to have a weekend of sleep than go on a vacation or getaway hoping to refresh oneself. Arianna, who had accidentally worked herself to exhaustion in 2007, subsequently became an evangelist for sleep. According to her, she only became successful when she started paying more attention to herself. She recounts,

"I can tell you with authority that when I'm exhausted, when I'm running on empty, I'm the worst version of myself," says the entrepreneur. "I'm more reactive. I'm less empathetic. I'm less creative. And all of us can testify to that."

You must ensure that you avoid burnouts in the course of your career. This is not only for health reasons; it is to ensure that you are able to reach your career aspirations. Burnouts can turn dreams into nightmares. Remember, the saddest part about things not working out is putting yourself at a point where you are unable to change it.

### Losing Your Job

Losing your job might not necessarily be a bad thing. More often than not, what happens to us in that season is dependent on us and how we manage the transition. The time spent in between jobs could either set you on a new promising path or lead you down an unfavourable path. The steps you take are critical to how you bounce back or if you bounce back.

Sometimes, losing your job might be a deliberate step on your part. I have often heard different reasons why people quit their jobs. You might have felt some of the things they felt.

They include;
1.    Inability to advance one's career.
2.    Toxic work environment.
3.    Stressful work pressure with resulting negative health implications.
4.    Feeling overqualified for the job.
5.    Lack of enthusiasm and excitement for the job role.

When exiting an organization, it is important to do so in a memorable and well-mannered way. In the case where you are leaving your job, you should remember to tender your resignation letter, return company property, and you may even ask for a recommendation letter. Endeavour to leave gracefully and without rebuking the workplace. Making an arrogant exit or leaving negative remarks behind offers no value for you and could potentially harm a future opportunity. This also applies when the organization terminates your employment. When many companies lay off workers, it is usually either because they find you incompetent or they are financially incapable of retaining your service. There may be other reasons, but these are the most popular.

A good way to approach your career when it has taken such pause is not to jump into a new adventure. Rather, you should spend some time evaluating yourself, especially to ensure you can do enough to either end up in a place that fits rightly with your passion or is appreciative of your skills. Of course, you may take random jobs if it is important for your financial stability. However, the more important thing is to do your best to guard against unfavourable termination of your job by putting yourself in a better position for your future endeavours. Losing your job can be an opportunity to start again, this time more appropriately. Thus, as much as losing your job may weigh you down, the faster you let go of the blues, examine yourself and put yourself out there to kick-start your career again, the better.

SECTION FOUR
# Factors that Influence
# Career Growth.

CHAPTER SEVEN

# VOLUNTEERING

*"If our hopes of building a better and safer
world are to become more than wishful thinking,
we will need the engagement of volunteers more than ever."*
— **Kofi Annan**

One of Florence's fondest memories was when she volunteered with Kate as part of the organizing committee for a quiz competition for girls during their university days. She had never felt more energized. The hours she spent with other volunteers in preparation for the quiz competition were some of her best. She remembered how they sat in the evening, after lectures, in one of the school's football fields, discussing how best to design the event. When it came to sending out proposals, she was at the forefront. She was happy to use her skills in writing the letters. She was quick to follow up on the proposals, and leapt for joy when she got a positive feedback on any. She realized that the event gave her two things; the chance to plan a meaningful event and see it work and the chance to make an impact on the lives of those girls. These were two joys that would not desert her.

That was also when she became friends with Kate. Kate's tenacity was inspiring. Due to their commitment to the event, both of them often found themselves working together as most of the buck stopped with them. While it could be overwhelming, they found support in each other and were glad to have the opportunity to work on something they both enjoyed. They called each other frequently and went about their assignments together. Those periods brought them together in ways they could never have imagined. It kicked off a lifetime of friendship which both of them were continuously grateful for.

The event had sparked a light in Kate. She had never felt more alive. This was the reason she started her own initiative, the Kate Project. She shared her feelings with Florence who was quick to encourage her on the new adventure. Since Kate floated her own initiative, Florence soon found that one of the most exciting times of her year was when she joined Kate in December for the end of year events where beneficiaries of the initiative present some of the works they had done throughout the year. Those times inadvertently brought memories of times past. She was also usually happy to see the women present some of their works after yearlong trainings. For Kate, she could not have been more grateful for the volunteering experience that pointed her in the direction of a career she was happy to pursue.

Whether you are seeking to give back to the community, make a difference in the lives of people around you, develop new skills or build on existing experience and knowledge, volunteering provides you with amazing opportunities. Also, volunteering allows you to spend quality time away from your everyday job, meet new people, make new friends, socialize and work pro bono.

I consider my volunteering experience to be an important part of my journey. What started off with a simple conversation about a book I had read led to a volunteer experience at a Knowledge Centre back in 2003. That experience exposed me to hundreds of books which I could read for free and a network of people whom I would never have had access to that early on in my career. While the foundation of my career might have started much earlier, my work at the Knowledge Centre proved to be an important starting point. It gave me the confidence to pursue a master's degree; I enrolled in a distant learning course that put me in the same class with serving ministers and military generals in Nigeria at the time. It was one of the most enlightening periods of my life, and the insights I got remain invaluable. It was during this period a group of development professionals gave me an exposé into the nonprofit world, which eventually led to my interest and work at ActionAid International Nigeria.

ActionAid's vision is 'A World without Poverty'. The organization is on a mission to eradicate the inequities and injustices that cause poverty. Seemed like a match made in career heaven, an organization whose mission aligned with my personal mission and values. ActionAid further introduced me to the importance of volunteering as I offered myself up to be sent to another organization for a month, in support of a big annual event. This was where I realized that there are opportunities volunteering brings and by extension, its importance in building a career.

Volunteering can serve as a solid foundation to build your career. Whether you are starting a new job, seeking promotion, changing your job, or continuing your education, volunteering exposes you to opportunities to use your skills, refine them, and gain new ones. It provides you with an avenue to practice and perfect your skills and actually use them for real life situations, which could range from solving a problem to advancing the execution of clear solutions and strategies. This ultimately brings you closer to your career goals while giving you the opportunity to have a positive influence on the lives of others. Volunteering is a special way to give and gain.

There are times you will apply for a job and the employer desperately requires experience in a specific field to spur confidence enough to entrust you with an existing vacant role. Volunteering provides opportunities to gain such experiences with lower risks. When you excel in such roles, you put yourself in a better position to take on larger and riskier ones. Varda Konstam, a professor emerita in the Counselling and School of Psychology department at the University of Massachusetts, Boston, reported findings that suggest there is a significant association between volunteering and finding employment. Konstam, after he had carried out a survey of more than 200 unemployed young adults, found that those who volunteer, even for a minimal investment of time, were more likely to procure employment six months later. She concluded that those who volunteer seemed to have an edge over their counterparts. She also highlighted it was independent of their careers, skill set or demographic differences.

Here are additional benefits of volunteering.

## SHOW YOU CAN BE COMMITTED TO GOOD WORK

How important is having volunteering experience on your resume? According to Jane Finkle, a career consultant and founder of Career Visions, volunteering experience shows your interest in building community and the likelihood that you will be a good citizen in the workplace. Your genuine willingness to invest yourself in the service of others, especially without financial compensation, paints you in a good light with your employer. The employer deduces that you will be able to lend yourself to the work of the organization, especially when the values are clear and defined. It shows you are the kind of person who takes initiative and makes yourself useful in the environments you find yourself.

## AVOID GAPS IN YOUR RESUME

Another important thing volunteering does is that it helps you avoid gaps in your resume. You know how when you are compiling your resume, you find it difficult to add any other thing aside from your educational background and the few roles you have occupied? You want to have other relevant experience and volunteering fills that void. It creates multiple avenues to do good work in line with your career. When you commit to such work, you can easily add them to your career profile. In addition to this, volunteering lets employers know you are more than your academic qualification; that you can actually transfer knowledge gained in the classroom to real life situations. It may also save the employer some money that would have been otherwise used to prepare you for the new job, especially if your volunteering experience is in line with your new job requirements.

## GAIN NEW SKILLS

Gaining new skills is the hallmark of volunteering. It is one of the most beautiful ways volunteering pays you back for your time. These include soft and hard skills such as leadership, critical thinking, collaboration and teamwork, problem solving, communication and technical expertise.

## REFERENCES AND INTRODUCTIONS

Have you been trying hard to get references? It is common for new employers to require a reference before you can be offered a job. Sometimes, you need references to enjoy scholarships or complete your application to a reputable school. When you immerse yourself in the good work that volunteering requires, you quickly qualify for good notes from some of those who worked with you. These references or notes about your invaluable contribution can be the final piece of the jigsaw in your quest to access new opportunities. However, ensure that the people who make your references know enough about you to actually answer questions about your person. Not to mention, ensure you seek people's permission before enlisting them as your reference.

## BUILD YOUR OWN NETWORKS

Volunteering affords you the opportunity to build new networks, especially with people who care about the same causes that you care about. These are networks you will hardly find in your workplace or schools. The characteristic it has of making like-minded people to gravitate towards each other is one exceptional thing about volunteering.

If you are going to enjoy a fulfilling career, you will need to meet several people whose relationships are germane to advancing said career. Some of these people are ordinarily not within your reach and trying to reach them on your own might prove tedious. One way to circumvent this is by getting introductions from people you worked with while volunteering who might have a closer connection with the people you would like to meet.

At times, because of the network you will potentially build, there is a possibility of you getting your next job with one of the people you meet while volunteering. One of my acquaintances, Adeola, would not stop going on about how she got a job with an employer whose project she had volunteered on a year before. The employer had watched her closely and surmised that she would be a valuable addition to her company. Without having to do an interview or submit her resume, the role was offered to her. She continues to relish the joy from that experience and remains a great advocate of not only volunteering when you can, but committing fully to it when you do. What is worth doing at all is worth doing well.

## TRY NEW FIELDS OF WORK

When Bola, a colleague at work, wanted to explore a career in finance, she hoped to base her decision on something beyond what she read over the internet. She wanted to experience what it felt like before taking the leap. Was a career in finance something she would enjoy, especially after the excitement of starting had faded away? Would she be able to handle the numbers as much as she thought she could? Instead of taking a blind jump and hoping for the best, she took a friend's advice to volunteer at a local education initiative that needed someone to handle their accounts. Initially she was reluctant, but she soon realized that it provided her with an opportunity to test the waters before taking the plunge. After volunteering for about half a year, she was equipped to make a more informed decision. She found out she loved keeping the records but was not particularly interested in sourcing for funds. So she refined her desire and targeted a Certificate in Treasury (CerT) qualification instead. Her volunteering experience had provided an invaluable direction for her career and set her up to take on a field she was more suited for and happy to do.

Volunteering can be helpful to you too, especially when you use it as a tool to advance your career. Remember that the purpose of this book is to help you build a conscious career that is fulfilling as well as rewarding. Therefore, you must consider several of the concepts mentioned in this book as tools to aid you in reaching the peak of your career. If volunteering is such an important tool to help you move forward, it then stands to reason that you should take it seriously. Beyond that, you need to understand how to utilize it for your own progress.

## MEDITATION POINT

If you are actively seeking a new volunteering experience, you should ponder on these questions.

- What cause do I care about?
- What organizations are advancing these causes?
- How may I advance this cause in my current organization?
- What skills do I want to explore or develop?
- How much time can I contribute? Do I need flexible hours?
- What experiences and features am I looking out for? What are the must-haves and the nice-to-haves?
- What considerations do I need to make to commit to this organization or cause

It is quite natural to want to jump into volunteering after learning about the numerous benefits it can bring you. But hold on a second so you do not waste your time, talent and resources with nothing to show for it in the end. This book is about taking deliberate steps that can positively influence your career. Thus, while I encourage you to volunteer, try not to do it with only personal interests in mind (as that will be selfish). It is important that your choices concerning volunteering are refined. As a matter of fact, it is possible that you may need to contribute to causes that cannot be immediately tied to your career goals before finding those that can. Regardless, here is how to use volunteering as a tool to propel your career:

## VOLUNTEER FOR A CAUSE THAT YOU LIKE

There are thousands of causes that require the contributions of volunteers to thrive and advance. Blindly plunging into them just for the sake of improving your resume or appearing better before friends and employers might not provide the experience you want. Remember that while you are actively seeking to volunteer, these organizations are actively seeking serious volunteers too.

Thus, you must always remain in control of your time and talent. Do not throw yourself at just any organization. One of the first things to do is to examine the cause the organization in question is trying to advance and make sure it aligns with causes you care about. For example, if I care about educational causes, then I should look out for organizations that have education as their focus. I should not be applying to join the Red Cross. Rather, a UNESCO volunteering opportunity will be more appropriate for me to pursue. Thus, when seeking volunteering opportunities, look for organizations or projects that care about similar causes as you do. This will make the experience more fulfilling for you and will also get the best out of you.

## VOLUNTEER FOR AN ORGANIZATION THAT WILL USE YOUR TIME WISELY

There are perhaps hundreds of non-profit organizations advancing causes that interest you. When you choose an organization, ensure it is one that will maximize your time. For many of us, who already have a busy schedule at work and are in the middle of our career, lending ourselves to voluntary causes might be a huge task. Thus, when you commit to such causes, it only makes sense that you use your time wisely.

Some organizations do not have the right structures and will spend an inordinate amount of time trying to accomplish simple tasks. If you cannot help optimize their processes, it is better for you to seek a new organization to help you fulfil your desire to contribute effectively to the society through the cause of your choice.

## VOLUNTEER FOR AN ORGANIZATION THAT WILL USE YOUR TALENT WISELY

When seeking to join an organization, you must ensure the organization requires your talent or is willing to allow you to fill a role where you can learn and practice the new skills you desire. There is very little you can accomplish if you join an organization where you are just a gratuitous appendage. Nonprofit organizations often fall into the pit of having too many volunteers who contribute nothing to the organization.

This happens frequently because they are not paying to retain the services of these volunteers. Thus, the onus is on you who chose to volunteer with such an organization to fill a role where you can hone your talent or learn new skills during your active period in that organization.

Seek organizations that need your service or those where you can become better at your skills. If an organization does not provide that, it is better you find another to join.

## SET GOALS FOR YOURSELF DURING YOUR VOLUNTEERING EXPERIENCE

Although I already mentioned earlier that joining a cause should not be all about what you intend to get from it, when you set out to work on a voluntary project or a non-profit, you should set goals based on your intended accomplishments. Building a conscious career requires that you set your direction and constantly measure your progress along that direction. When you set goals, you give yourself a reference for measuring your progress. This will also ensure that you are not lost in the frenzy that sometimes accompanies joining a cause that positively affects the lives of others.

## VOLUNTEER WITHOUT PUTTING TOO MUCH STRAIN ON YOURSELF

One thing you want to avoid is lending yourself to an experience that burns you out and renders you incapable of fulfilling your other responsibilities, especially your paid work or time with your family, if you have one. If the volunteering opportunity is your only commitment, you may be more flexible. However, for those who combine volunteering with other important commitments, it is necessary to choose a volunteering opportunity that fits into your schedule.

There are some volunteer roles you can effectively do without leaving your home. A lot of organizations allow you to work with them remotely and online.

If you have constraints moving around, then you should consider these kinds of volunteer jobs. Volunteering should not place too much burden on you else, you will fail to enjoy it, provide your best or get the best out of it. Thus, while you may seek to change the world in more meaningful ways, if you cannot adapt it to your schedule, you must be able to refine your schedule to conveniently accommodate your new volunteering adventure.

## VOLUNTEER AT A PROJECT YOU CAN ACTUALLY CONTRIBUTE YOUR BEST

Join an organization where your contribution is meaningful, needed and recognized. Join a project where you can be at your best. Remember that volunteering is about giving, thus seek organizations where you can give your all. My mantra remains give your 100 percent or nothing. Going half-hearted into a project or cause benefits neither you nor the cause, so why do it? I trust that you have no desire to be lumped among the numbers. You want to stand out in any field you find yourself in.

Finally, if the opportunity presents, consider joining organizations that provide you with quality trainings and access to experienced persons who can provide support for your career. Your goal is to give your best to any cause you volunteer with while also getting the best from that experience. Some volunteering roles even offer stipends among other allowances to cover your expenses while rendering your service. You can actively seek out these ones too.
Regardless of your chosen option, you should understand that volunteering is based on altruism and actively seeking financial rewards interferes with that concept.

## GAP YEARS

I think introducing at least one gap year for students to take on volunteering work before being absorbed into tertiary institutions can help them make better career choices. While it may have worked for a lot of people to complete their academic experience before venturing into the work sphere, I think more people should consider taking breaks from academics to test the world of work through volunteering or internships, as this can actually help them make better career choices as they move forward into the universities. I believe this can reduce the population of people who find themselves unfulfilled at the end of their university education, because they somehow found that they do not like the courses they studied.

Generally, volunteering opportunities provide people with low pressure and friendly environments to discover themselves, become better at their work, and expand their networks, especially in fields that fuel their passion. Volunteering puts you in circles where you can engage in genuine and meaningful conversations with people who share similar interests. It is up to you to make the best of it.

CHAPTER EIGHT

# PEOPLE, PROCESS AND STRUCTURES

*"Whatever good things we build end up building us"*
**-Jim Rohn**

If there was anything Florence struggled with, it was understanding people. She felt that once you are able to show your value, you should not need to please people to get what you want. Truthfully, she had never had to do more than that to move up on her career ladder, but as she climbed higher it became much more difficult to rise without maintaining good relationships with people. She once relayed her frustration to Kate after her proposal to the company's management on the year's operation strategies was declined.

"Can you imagine, Kate, that after presenting what I believed to be the best strategy at the General Meeting, the management went with Mr John's? I agree that his proposal was good, but I guarantee that mine would have produced better results and at a lower cost."

"I am not surprised," Kate replied. "You've always pointed out that people should always be logical. But, they are not. We are all emotional and our emotions come to play when making decisions. Is it the same Mr John I met at your last luncheon you are referring to? I observed that he treats people specially. He just has a way of making people like him."

Florence shrugged, her disappointment apparent as she knew Kate was right. John does have a way with people that makes it easy for him to get what he wants, without exploiting them or going out of his way to please them. It was a quality she had started to realize its importance. She had always felt people would only act based on logical reasons. She soon realized her assumption was wrong when it dawned on her that the only reason she stops at a particular woman's stall on her trips to the market, instead of her neighbor's stall that offers similar items, is because the woman has a pleasant disposition.

Having discussed the process of setting goals and understanding how to prepare ourselves for the current and future world of work, it is important to discuss other requirements that are essential for you to achieve your set goals. In this chapter, we will explore how to take advantage of relationships, processes and structures - whether good or bad, to move you towards your desired career goals. This book will aid your career growth, but note that your ability to successfully navigate relationships, processes and structures are necessary requirements to move you forward.

**PEOPLE**

People are everywhere. They are behind the deals we want to make and the impact we intend to create. They can make a short journey tortuous and a long journey unbearable or otherwise. As we move along on our career journey, we will need to interact with several people. These people can make or mar our plans of building a fulfilling and financially rewarding career. Trying to build a career without interacting with people is not possible. Therefore, the logical thing to do is to understand how to build better relationships with people, both to help you remove people obstacles, as well as to help you build productive partnerships.

Understanding how to relate with people does not mean you have to go out of your way to please people or build relationships with everyone you meet. It just means you are able to identify people who are important to your progress, those who are not and how to maintain the right relationships with all these people.

As I mentioned earlier, people are made up of boxes of emotions. Therefore, the best way to relate with people is built on the foundation of understanding their emotions. While we may understand other people's emotions, we also need to understand our own emotions, and then be able to bridge the gap between ourselves and other people. This phenomenon is called Emotional Intelligence.

According to Daniel Goleman, "Emotional Intelligence (EQ) is defined as the ability to identify, assess, and control one's own emotions, the emotions of others, and that of groups." This ability to learn what people are feeling helps us do things that inspires them to act in favourable ways. Note that this is not the same as manipulating people. In his book, Goleman divided Emotional intelligence into five sections:

1.   **SELF-AWARENESS:** It starts with knowing your emotions, strengths, weaknesses, drives, values and goals and to recognize their impact on others.

2.   **SELF-REGULATION:** This is your ability to manage or redirect one's disruptive emotions and impulses and adapt to changing circumstances. While no one has a perfect demeanor, it is important to strive towards becoming a better version of ourselves. This includes controlling emotions that may produce negative consequences.

3.   **SOCIAL SKILL:** Managing other people's emotions to stir them in the desired direction. When you are working with a team, you become a unit of a social group. Your ability to maintain your status as a functional unit of that group, while fulfilling your role, means you have good social skills. Social skills are what you use to interact and communicate, both verbally and non-verbally, with other members of **a group.**

4.   **EMPATHY:** You should be able to recognize, understand, and consider other people's feelings, especially when making decisions. People consider it disrespectful, inconsiderate and harsh when you take actions without considering their feelings. It makes them unwilling to interact with you and more willing to bear a grudge. They are less likely to collaborate with you, whether or not you are doing something valuable and impactful.

5.   **MOTIVATION:** Learning how to motivate oneself to achieve a goal for the sake of achievement, using both intrinsic and extrinsic motivation. This is one of the most important things to consider when relating with people. When dealing with a person, you must ask yourself, what is this person's motivation? What drives this person? What gets this person excited? If you figure this out, it becomes easier to relate with that person by motivating them correctly. You know how giving an instruction only to a kid and giving an instruction with a sweet, or some other form of a treat, to a kid works differently? That is what I am talking about.

Gaining mastery of Emotional Intelligence allows you to relate with people much better. It makes you a better unit within a social group. It makes you a better person and makes it more likely for you to reach your goal of a fulfilling and financially rewarding career.

**MEDITATION POINT**

A good way to go about understanding the people, process and structures question is to ask yourself these questions:

- WHO is instrumental to my journey to build my desired career?
- HOW do I go about my journey to build my desired career?
- WHAT do I need to put in place to build my desired career?

Aside from improving your emotional intelligence, a trait which can be learned, you should also avoid making assumptions about people's characters and labelling them. Instead, you should strive to learn more about these people and know why they act the way they do. This lets you know what to do to improve a situation when dealing with such people. In addition, it is necessary to acknowledge that people are different. Appreciating these differences makes it easier for you to relate with people and allows you to understand that perspectives around a single subject can differ and the way people react to certain situations also differs.

If you succeed in getting people on your side, getting to the peak of your career becomes a walk in the park.

## NETWORKING

I assume this is not your first time of hearing this word. Connecting with other people is one of the most important aspects of anyone's career. At the base of every successful career is a foundation of connections. However, my definition of networking differs slightly from the conventional definition. I believe that life allows you to network naturally and building a career makes networking a more fluid process, especially if you are building a conscious career which will most like bring you before people you share similar values and interests with.

There are several times you come across certain opportunities and you struggle to think of anyone in your circle that is qualified for them. Eventually, you let it slip through or simply just broadcast it, hoping it finds a lucky person. In a similar way, people are usually in a situation where they do not remember you when an opportunity you are fit to have comes to their desk. The reason for this is that you have not properly connected with them on a level where they are aware and confident of your abilities. Also, remember that people are unwilling to recommend people they do not know, because they do not want to put their own integrity on the line. When you properly understand this, it makes it easier to understand the value in connecting with people and creating meaningful relationships. You also begin to acknowledge how important networking and connecting with the right people is for your career.

Information moves in circles. Despite the fact that the world is becoming more open and connected, privileged information (which is information that could be important to your career growth), moves in specific circles, and hardly goes out of that circle. Therefore, it is possible that some opportunity you have always wanted, such as a sponsored travel to England for a conference to present your academic paper on renewable energy, is floating within a circle of people who are unable to use that opportunity but whom you do not have access to.

Maybe all of these people hold key positions in renewable energy companies and/or nonprofits working in that space. The chance of you getting that information is very minimal if you are not in that circle. Also, what public announcement on the opportunity presents might not be enough to guide you to access or take advantage of the opportunity. Not being part of a circle could cost you and deprive you of a career opportunity as we saw in the case of Florence above.

Does it mean you have to belong to almost all the circles, and become friends with almost anyone you see? Definitely not! Aside from the fact that this is too daunting a task to take on, it is also fruitless. Instead, what you do is conscious networking. When meeting a new person or establishing a new relationship, understand why that person or relationship is important. What role will this new relationship play in my journey? Your goal should be to connect with circles where information that leads to your career progress are likely to be shared. It is still quite possible that you still miss out on certain opportunities, but you are likely to have access to more than you would have if you were not deliberate in networking.

Let me just clarify that networking is not sharing business cards. Ask yourself, how many business cards do you keep and how many have you actually used. A business card should be issued mostly after you have built the right connection with the other person. Some people go to events armed with business cards, with the intent of just giving it to people, hoping to get lucky by having one of those people call them. That rarely happens. So, save yourself the trouble and instead of aiming to have your business card in everyone's pocket, aim to leave an impression that makes it difficult for the other person to forget you, such that when an opportunity presents itself, you are immediately the first person that comes to mind.

This implies that the people must not only know you, they must also be able to vouch for you. For that to happen, it means they must trust you and your abilities. Networking for networking sake will get you nowhere. It has to be a conscious effort to create meaningful relationships with different circles of people in and out of your profession.

In the same vein, you must be willing to contribute to the circles that you connect with. I remember my late friend, Tare, who was a pro at contributing to different circles by always volunteering to serve on the committee of almost every association she belonged to. This became her channel to doing the significant work she did before she died and it was evident at her funeral where these different groups came to pay tribute to her, her work and the life of service she lived.

The American author and world record holder, Lewis Howes, was quoted to have said,

"One of the most powerful networking practices is to provide immediate value to a new connection. This means the moment you identify a way to help someone, take action."

As you build your network and grow in your career, you will meet different people who will play different roles in your career. I have tried to classify them below:

**Facilitators/Sponsors** – These are people who make direct contributions to your career to help you move forward. Some of them may be colleagues, relatives, friends or mentors. They enable you and are keen to see you progress and will take actions when they can to help you.

**Inhibitors** – These people make it difficult for you to move forward, sometimes without even being aware of it themselves. When you meet these kind of people, do not be discouraged. Instead, seek ways to understand what their main issues are or what interests you share in common and work at making the relationship better. This will help build your emotional intelligence quotient. However, if it does not work out, find a way out of the relationship. But, ensure that if you are guilty of any behavior or act you are accused of, you work on them.

**Influencers** – These are people who you do not necessarily come in contact with, but have an impact on the way you want to live your life and build your career. Many times, influencers are successful in the field you are pursuing.

Aside from being successful, they have been exemplary and have gone through similar challenges you are facing, or will face. Thus, they inspire you to do more and reach for the summit of your career. They show you possibilities of what you could be and what can be overcome.

**Cheerleaders** – These are supporters who provide moral support. They are neither in the capacity to help you directly, nor will they go out of their way to help you if they could. Yet, they are excited about your progress and will continue to cheer you on. One important mistake you should avoid is to mistake a cheerleader for an enabler. People might be excited about your progress but that does not automatically mean they are willing to invest or contribute to seeing you progress.

**Implementers** – These are people who are keen to act and execute the ideas you share with them. They form good teammates especially if you seek to work on a new project or create a team.

**PROCESSES**

When building a conscious career, you should be able to understand the process you will need to undertake to reach your career goals. You should identify how you will go about it, what steps you need to take and by when. Processes are not plans. Rather, they are maps that allow you to understand your journey better. Creating a process document will provide you with an overview of what you need to do and whether you are capable of doing them. It is like mapping out your journey, as if you can see the future. This exercise is important because it informs your choice of employers as you embark on your journey and if they have complimentary processes that will help you achieve what you have mapped out

This is not a speculative assignment. Many people have built careers similar to what you want to build. All you have to do is to make the right enquiries from the right people. These days, you may even complete your entire research online without speaking to anyone. But, you should find someone to talk to as several times, secrets that could aid your career growth may not be available online.

For example, if I want to be a professional mechanical engineer, my processes can be:

- Get a degree in Mechanical Engineering.
- Become a Graduate member of the Nigerian Society of Engineers.
- Master three design softwares (Autocad, SolidWorks and CATIA).
- Work for two years in a Mechanical Engineering Firm.
- Get a Masters in Structural Analysis.
- Get a COREN Certification.
- Attend five Engineering conferences.
- Work for five years as a Structural Engineer.
- Go for a doctorate degree.

A process is simply the course of action you need to take to achieve a particular result. It is the foundation on which you build your plan. The difference between a plan and a process is that a process shows you how to do it, while a plan is a description of how and when you will do it.

If you do not understand the processes required to reach your goals, then it becomes difficult to plan properly. Although I acknowledge that things can change, it is better to plan to give yourself the best chance at building a fulfilling career, then learn to adapt your processes quickly to the changes and your reality as it happens. Nothing is set in stone. You must remain nimble and flexible.

**STRUCTURES**
Structures are what you need to put in place or need to be in place for you to achieve your results. Your structures are those things or people that makes reaching your goals more feasible. Your structures are your support.

One important structure is finance. Money plays a significant role in enabling career progress. While it is possible to move forward with minimal funding, for some of the experiences and knowledge you may want to gather, you will need financial support. Thus, after you may have understood the process to reaching your career goals, it becomes important to understand the structures you have to put in place to enable you go through the process.

The importance of getting reliable sources of information about your field cannot be underrated. This helps to keep you in the loop at all times. You may end up going in the wrong direction very fast if you do not have access to the right information. Curate things, places and people who you know can provide adequate support for your career and always stay in touch with them.

For married people who are seeking career advancements that may affect their family life, it is important to find the right support structure whether in form of family, temporary, permanent, paid or unpaid help to ensure the family does not suffer. When you make provisions for this, you are putting in place structures that will enable you grow your career.

Therefore, as you get a clearer picture of your career journey and how to get there, you should seek what you will require at each stage to be able to continue progressing. People, processes and structures are enablers of your career success. But, how you maximize them is what determines how effectively they will work for you.

CHAPTER NINE

# FINANCIAL EDUCATION
# AND NEGOTIATION

*"There is a secret psychology of money.*
*Most people don't know about it.*
*That's why most people never become financially successful.*
*A lack of money is not the problem;*
*it is merely a symptom of what's going on inside of you."*

**-T. Harv Eke**

It was when Kate finally opened up to her friend, Florence, that she realized how poor Kate had been with her finances. Even though Kate did not earn that much money, Florence felt she could be more careful with how she managed the money she did make. Her poor understanding of how money works had made it difficult for her to improve her financial status.

"You need to learn more about money," Florence told her. "I am not saying you should change your focus from making impact but if you do not learn about it, you might find it difficult to do some of the things you want to do…like making more impact."

"What is there to learn about money?" Kate wondered, "I just need to make enough money so I can cater to my needs. And I am not making enough money. That is what we have to solve."

This was not the first time Florence had heard those words. When she spoke with several of her friends or colleagues about money, most of them retorted that they just needed to make more money. Yet, Florence knew that making more money was not going to happen if they did not change their spending habit and learn more about money. Her colleagues often wondered how she lived a more comfortable life than they did despite them having higher wages. It was simple; Florence had cultivated a disciplined approach to money since she became financially literate. She continued to read more on how to become better with money and maximize every income that would come her way. She wondered why numerous people were so careless about something that is important to their well-being, but it turns out they did not know better.

In order to build a financially rewarding career, you need to understand how money works. You need to know how to multiply your income. The fact that you have limited number of hours to work each day can make you think that your ability to earn much more than you currently do is just as limited. However, this is not true. It is also not true that once you focus on your passion and excel in it, money will automatically flow in. It is important that as you become better in your career, you become better in the business side of it.

If you do not pay attention to this part, it can affect the overall fulfilment you are aiming for in the end.

Learning about the financial part of your career is being financially literate. When you educate yourself financially, it not only helps you, it also helps the economy of your country of residence. One book that has influenced many people's attitude to money, especially successful ones, is Rich Dad, Poor Dad by Robert Kiyosaki. According to him, rich people know how money works. They understand how to spend money. And most importantly, they know how to make money work for them.

Although lack of financial understanding is the reason people are poor at saving and go into avoidable debts, financial literacy goes beyond just saving and avoiding debt. Financial literacy encompasses the understanding of how to multiply your assets and minimize your liabilities. Note that I did not mention how much you make in a month, because what matters most is the habit and not the amount. If your plan to get rich is to multiply the number of hours you work, you might burn out. Similarly, if your plan is to do little and get more money in return, you might continue to live a fantasy. My approach to a financially rewarding career is to think differently about money while providing the best value. Here are tips that will help you to create financial stability as you build your career.

1.      See the world in abundance

A great place to start is to examine how you think about the world generally. Do you think about the world as a place of scarcity or a place full of abundance? The idea that there is not enough to go round eventually limits our aspiration for a financially rewarding career. A wrong approach to adopt is the belief that someone else must lose for you and others to gain. This is not always true. We can all get more from life without shortchanging others. It is not a zero sum game. You must start thinking about the world in terms of abundance. There is enough to go round if we all provide enough value to capture it.

You must believe that there is enough wealth to go round and that you have the capacity to gain from it. You must start seeing the world in abundance. When you do, you are more mentally prepared for a financially rewarding career.

## 2.      No overnight success

Having a financially rewarding career does not mean you will start to look for means to cut corners. If you will build wealth that lasts, I advise that you build on a credible and strong foundation, and this usually takes some time to do. While you keep your mind on your career goals, you should keep your eyes peeled on doing the daily work. As you put the bricks together, it will eventually come together. You know what they say; a house hurriedly built is set for doom.

Thus, if you cannot immediately see the result of your work, do not let it demotivate you. Instead, ensure you are following the process you have laid out to enable you reach your goals. Enjoy the quick and small wins that come with everyday progress. When you fall short, re-calibrate, re-strategize and get moving again. Remember the old adage; Quitters never win, Winners never quit. If you keep going, you will eventually get there.

## 3.      Learn How to Create and Capture Value

The road to financial gain is quite simple; it revolves around creating and capturing value. The value you create is your skill, product, service or the money you give out for a certain event while the value you capture is the skill, product, service or money you get in return. It is all about completing that circle of exchange. A positive exchange is giving out what is less valuable to you at a time to someone who has something that is more valuable to you. For example, I have a pair of designer shoes. While this is valuable, I believe I could get something even more valuable for it; which is money. Thus, I offer the shoe to someone who values the shoe more than the money they will exchange for it. In the end, both parties are happy. I have got something more valuable to me, while the other person has got something more valuable to her.

Creating value in exchange for value is how the standard world of business works. Thus, your ability to provide value for people who are willing to give you something more valuable to you, because what you offer them is more valuable to them, is one of the fundamental ways of creating wealth.

What this means is; when creating value, you must seek people who are willing to pay you appropriately. This is called finding your target audience. When you create value for people who do not recognize the benefit of the value you are creating, you are likely to be underpaid or not paid at all. This is because the person on the other end does not think what you are giving is valuable enough to give you what you want in return. Now, this is different from a situation where a person clearly does not have the capability to pay you due to financial constraints despite recognizing the value you bring to the table.

Your goal should be to find people who have the capacity to pay you and also recognize the value you can give to them. Sometimes, people are oblivious to what is valuable to them. In such cases, you must be able to sell your value to those who need it. Finding your target audience is not enough, your ability to sell your value is just as critical.

One of my friends makes quality leather shoes. She struggled with sales and her shop was filled with unsold shoes. It depressed her so much. When she consulted with me, I asked her what the problem was. Her response was,

"People are simply buying synthetic leather shoes instead, which are cheaper. I had to stop making the shoes since no one was buying them. Even when I dropped the price below the cost price, I only got a few buys. Please help me."

I told her to look for the right market.

"That the leather shoes are valuable to you, does not mean they are valuable to other people. Even when you find your audience, you must be able to tell them why your shoes will be a great buy."

Another example was when Olaide, a former colleague who now works as the Project Manager of an event management company, learned new project management ideas and struggled to introduce them to her new firm. Because Olaide was tech savvy, she was able to use several project management tools like Asana and Trello, as well as effective project management methods like the Kanban. She had thought that introducing such new ways would improve their productivity at work and eventually lead to her promotion. Imagine her shock when this did not happen. Instead, her colleagues were unhappy as it seemed she was trying to create more problems for them by making them learn how to use new tools and methods that were different from their current tools and methods.

Rather than appreciate her for her inventiveness, her colleagues became hostile towards her. Olaide was not only unhappy, she did not get the promotion and pay rise she wanted. While she had blamed her colleagues when she complained to me, I felt she could have employed a different approach to win over her colleagues and get them to use products and processes that would have clearly improved their productivity and eased their tasks. Her inability to sell her value to her audience (her colleagues) meant that she could not get what she wanted in return. It could also be that she had approached the wrong people in the organization to adopt her ideas.

There is no standard measurement for value, as it is subjective. Aluminium spoons used to be more expensive than silver spoons. Now, they are one of the most common and perhaps least expensive type of spoons in the market. Did aluminium stop being aluminium? No! But the value people ascribed to aluminium subsequently changed for reasons best known to them.

When you create value but you do not sell it to the right market, you might encounter financial frustration. You will be constantly undervalued. However, when you are in the right market, offering the right value, you become prized. Thus, if you currently feel undervalued, what you should do is to be on the look-out for a place where your value is needed and consequently, better appreciated. When you find and fit yourself into this place, you will experience a positive change in your career.

On the other hand, it is possible you have seen the potential in a particular market or with a particular audience, and all you have to do is modify your value to fit that market. For example, if you are a fashion designer and you feel the need to cater to the mass market, what you have to do is figure out how you can modify your production to allow you serve this market. This can include changing your price to increase affordability. It can be using materials that can withstand poor handling and ensuring you cut out all processes that can spike your product cost.

When you do this, the people in this market will appreciate your value more and be willing to pay for the clothes you make at your new price. You probably will make as much money serving a hundred people in the mass market as you would if you were serving one client in the high-end market. Everyone goes home happy.

The same rules apply in the workplace. You should seek to understand what is valuable to your organization so you know if you fit in and what you need to do to be appreciated. A company will pay more for someone they feel is more valuable to them. That is why you sometimes see your boss spend more on a certain project though she has complained of limited finance to support your own project. Seek to understand your value chain and try to create the right value to capture more value from the chain.

To get optimum value out of your work, ask these questions:

- Am I obtaining the right value for the services I am offering?
- Am offering my services in the right place?
- Is there a way I can create more value for the people I am serving?
- What things am I spending time on that is not creating the right value for the people I am serving?
- What is the value to the people/organisation am serving and how can I focus my capabilities on them?
- How can I obtain more value for the services I am offering?

We all offer service. If you are an entrepreneur, you serve your customers and your stakeholders. If you are an employee, you serve your employer.

### 4.    Coordinate Your Expenses

The first step to coordinating money you have acquired is identifying how you should spend it. Money is a means to an end, but you must apply it to the right ends if you do not want to encounter financial frustration. What is taking your money away?

I once heard a good description of financial mismanagement. The person said it was like pouring water into a sink with many drains. If you want to stop the waste, the obvious thing to do is identify the drains and block them. But you cannot block them if you do not first identify them. In line with this, your first step to financial management is tracking your expense. What are you spending money on? When you document this, you will understand your personal cash flow and be empowered to do something about it if it worries you.

You can't improve what you don't measure.

The next step is to control your expenses. If you do not learn to control your expenses, it will not matter if you earn more. This is because you are likely to continue spending more than you earn, leaving you in a state of financial worry. The ultimate goal of a financially educated person is to spend below their means.

**QUICK EXERCISE**
Take a note and create a table. One column should be titled Expenses and the other should be titled Amount. Now use this simple table to document everything you spend your money on over the next one month. When you return to this book after a month, review your expenses and try to see if you are spending the right amount on the right things and find ways to further maximize your expenditure.

5.      **Understand the difference between an asset and a liability**

In Robert Kiyosaki's book, Rich Dad Poor Dad, the author highlighted the significant difference between assets and liabilities. The rich have a greater advantage over the poor because they understand this difference. While the focus of this book is not to explain wealth gaps, it is critical for people who aspire to have a prosperous career to learn more about their assets and liabilities. This is especially so that they can build more assets in their careers and lower their pile of liabilities efficiently.

Simply put, an asset is something that brings more money to you while liabilities are things that take money away from you. Everyone has both assets and liabilities, although in different proportions. Your ability to tilt the balance in favour of assets is what provides you financial independence. If you enjoy your liabilities so much, e.g. luxury cars, designer products, expensive holidays, spa treats and so on, the question you need to ask yourself is - what assets do I need to acquire to ensure I can continue to enjoy these liabilities? Doing this will protect you from being broke at the end of your career when you can no longer work.

### 6.    Save

One of my favourite books, The Richest Man in Babylon by George Samuel Clason about financial education, advices that you keep one tenth of your earnings as savings. When you save money, you prepare yourself for the uncertain future. Since the future is always uncertain, then it makes sense to always save. When you know you are financially stable and can withstand any eventualities in the immediate future, you are more willing to go after your dreams. You are also happier when you know there is money in the bank.

### 7.    Invest

"Remember that money is of a prolific generating nature. Money can beget money, and its offspring can beget more." – Benjamin Franklin

Learning to save money is not enough. If you want to earn more income than your work gives you, then you should let your money make more money for you. This is mostly possible by investing. However, you should be careful when investing your money. There are all sorts of schemes out there and if you do not take care, you will be thrown headlong into financial frustration. The first rule of investing is this; do not invest in something you know little about. When you invest in what you understand, you are likely to know the accompanying risks, their magnitude and therefore, you can properly protect yourself against them. When you don't, you are at the whims of the market and you will most likely lose.

My advice is; take risks but make sure they are calculated ones. A good method to adopt is consulting with an experienced investor. Remember to also start small. This helps you build your confidence as you achieve small wins before you throw yourself all in. It also reduces the cost of your mistakes. Although you are never fully covered from loss when investing, you can reduce the likelihood of losing when you are smart about your investments.

### 8.    Insure your priciest possessions

The loss of some of our possessions can throw us off the financial ladder and send us back to square one. What smart people do is get insurance cover for these possessions against unforeseen occurrences.

This makes you more financially stable and leaves you rest assured and confident that you can weather storms that come.

### 9.      Plan for your retirement

When we build wealth, we worry less about the pressures of life and can focus on building a career and planning for retirement. Creating retirement securities for yourself only adds more rocks to the foundation of your financial stability. It is preferable to be wealthy enough that you do not need your retirement payback than it is to end up without one. There are many retirement plans you can enjoy from pension fund managers. All you need to do is set aside a portion of your income to be put in your retirement savings.

### 10.  Reduce the loss of your money.

According to Robert Kiyosaki, there are four things that can take money away from you. These are taxes, inflation, debt and retirement. As you become more financially literate, your goal should be to understand how these money drains work, so you can learn how to effectively mitigate them. As a matter of fact, you should aim at gaining more knowledge on how these money-drains can make you even more money.

### NEGOTIATION

As I close this chapter, I find it necessary to discuss how to get the best out of deals you enter.

You will often find yourself trying to negotiate a transaction, deal or contract agreement. Since you do not usually know what the other person knows or thinks, you end up being nervous and trying not to get on the wrong side of the negotiation. Before I share tips on how to get the best out of negotiations, I will differentiate between a bad negotiation and a good one.

A bad negotiation is one in which one or two of either party gets out of the negotiation feeling undervalued. All parties should come out of a negotiation feeling good about the deals they arrived at.

Thus, my tips are about making good negotiation decisions where all parties involved, including you, get what makes them happy:

### 1.   Be Patient
A negotiation is not something you want to jump in and out of. Whether you are negotiating a salary with an employer or equity with an investor, learn to be patient. This will prevent you from making a hasty decision that you eventually regret. Never be in a hurry to close a deal.

### 2.   Understand your cost of entering the deal
A good way to come out happy in a deal is to ensure that you do not commit yourself to an agreement where you end up putting in more than you gain. If you are reviewing your salary with your boss or terms of a contract, think about what it will take to deliver on that role or on the job. When you know the full cost of your commitment, it gives you a proper perspective into what you should accept and what you should not.

### 3.   Be Confident
Look calm and assured. Avoid appearing desperate at all cost. This is to prevent the other party from taking advantage of your situation. You must always act like you have other options and can walk away from the deal if it does not favour you. This is especially important when taking on a new job. When the employer sees that you are desperate to accept the job, they might take advantage of this, and try to pay you lower than you would ordinarily accept.

### 4.   Listen
Pay attention to the other party involved in the negotiation. Seek to know what makes a good deal for the other party and identify their core interest. This is important because you are most likely to close the deal if and when the other party is satisfied with it. Negotiation should be based on mutual understanding. When both parties are happy about the deal made, none of them would eventually try to cut corners after the agreement.

### 5. Ask Questions

When you are unclear about some of the offers or terms the other party puts forward, ask questions. This way, you can avoid hinging your decisions on the wrong information.

### 6. Be Prepared

You should be clear about the value you bring to the table and the value you hope to capture from the deal. You must communicate this effectively during the course of negotiation and not repeatedly switch decisions. Also, ensure you and the other party, are clear on what the deal is about and what you hope to get out of it.

### 7. Make Concessions on the appropriate Values.

You can reach a mutually beneficial conclusion in negotiations by making smart trade-offs. This means conceding on things you value less but the other party values highly, while proposing the other party makes a concession on something you value highly that she values less. Getting a job that gives you more free time to spend with your family in exchange for less money is an example of this in the context of your career.

### 8. Read about Negotiation

Learn more about negotiation from books that have been written specifically about the subject. Some of them are Getting More by Stuart Diamond, Bargaining for Advantage by Richard Shell, and Getting to Yes by Roger Fisher et al.

### SOLVING KATE'S DILEMMA

Kate needs to become financially literate and understand the business side of her passion. If she focuses on her initiative full time, then she must begin to pay herself. Kate needs to realize that her wellbeing is important to the success of her business. Financial stability frees up the mind for more productivity and creativity.

Another option Kate can explore is cutting down on the number of hours she spends on her initiative and taking on an extra job.

This will ensure she is financially healthy while she also spends some hours tending to her passion.

For Kate to be able to pay herself, she needs to learn more about the opportunities that may benefit her initiative. These include grants and donations. She can set her organization up to enjoy some of these financial support schemes in order to increase her impact as well as ensure her wellbeing. She may also set her initiative up to be a social enterprise. This way, it can depend on the returns it gets from commercial activities.

When Kate is able to save money, either from her work or from the works of the initiative, she should consider putting some funds in low risk investments. Time is a great multiplier of money when kept in the right investments. Kate can then gain from the compounding returns from her investment and become more financially stable. Kate's ability to keep her passion going is critical to her emotional fulfilment. Her ability to stay ahead of money worries would guarantee her financial fulfilment.

## SOLVING FLORENCE'S DILEMMA

Florence's financial education has put her on a steady path to financial fulfilment at the end of her career. However, her longing for emotional fulfilment is a void that needs urgent attention. Florence needs to identify her passion and create a plan that allows her go after it.

To begin, she should look within the organization she currently works for and see what kind of value she can create for the organization which they will appreciate and is also in line with her passion. Whether through intrapreneurship or through corporate social responsibility, Florence should sit with her boss and discuss how her passion may bring value to the organization, if allowed.

Alternatively, if Florence is unable to reconcile her passion with her current job, she has two options. One is to leave the job for a more fulfilling one. The other is to pursue her passion outside office hours. This calls for a more disciplined approach to time management.

While I will normally recommend that you pursue a career that fulfils both your financial and emotional needs, I also understand that it is different strokes for different people. Therefore, make the best decision for yourself each and every time without losing the essence of who you are.

SECTION FIVE

# Moving Forward - Building A Conscious Career

## CHAPTER TEN

# TAKING ACTION

*"Do or do not, there is no try"*

*- Joda*

As I proceed to the end of this book, I certainly hope you have learnt the how of intentionally building a fulfilling career that is also financially rewarding. The journey is a long one and I can tell you that, more often than not, it is not an easy one. As with anything else in life, when you attempt to go the extra mile, it usually comes with challenges. The good thing is; it is nothing you cannot overcome if you set your mind to it. Therefore, what you have learnt so far is to guide you to make actionable plans and take practical steps towards building a fulfilling career. But nothing starts until you take action, so everything we have done in the last nine chapters of this book has been to get us to this point where you can take action. My hope is that you feel so energized from reading this book, and you put everything into practice. The lessons in this book will only yield results if you apply them to your career.

Taking action comes with a lot of effort and dedication, but it is the only way to get your desired results. Taking action can mean taking the leap or continuing in your current stead. It might mean reviewing everything you have known and have been doing all this while and taking steps to change them for good. It might mean re-allocating your time, leaving your job, going back to school, leaving school or having a sit down with your employer or team. Whatever taking action means for you, you must start now. There is no better time than the present.

## PARTING SHOTS

While I have shared a lot of the lessons I have learnt while building my career, I do not claim that my list of things to do to build a fulfilling and financially rewarding career is exhaustive by any length. Therefore, you must continue to read, seek advice and filter through everything you hear while making the best decisions for your career. I believe these parting shots, along with every other thing you have learnt in this book, can guide you as you go ahead to make your career one that you, and the people around you who will be impacted, can be incredibly proud of.

## TAKING RISKS

If you seek to reach farther than most people will ever reach in their careers, you cannot avoid taking risks. You will be in several situations where you have to make a decision that seems crazy and unrealistic. The average person will warn you against it. But, within yourself, if you feel the conviction that it could lead to a big break, then by all means, go for it. I cannot say I know all the situations you will ever be in, what I do know is that the world's most successful people did not get to their peak by being too careful. Still, it is worthy of note to state that while taking risks, you should understand what you are going to face, and be sure you can withstand the outcome if it does not go your way. Even more, take calculated risks.

## ON FAILING

The reason many people never reach beyond their current realities is that they are afraid of failing. At this stage of my career, I have undergone several challenges that proved too difficult for my capability sometimes. But I never let that hinder my career goals. I will not go deeply into how to react to failure as I believe by now, you know failing is a part of growing. What I will like to share is something I learnt very early on in my career. When you fail, you should ask yourself two important questions.

- What did I do right?
- What could I have done better?

If you notice, these two questions are forward thinking. They are about getting better and moving forward. The worst thing you can do to yourself is holding firmly to the past or the part of you that failed. You should not waste your time blaming yourself or your environment. Your focus should always be on the goal. You should constantly be thinking – How do I move closer to my goal?

This method has worked for me several times and ensured I moved forward faster. I agree that the magnitude of setbacks vary across different situations and with different people, but regardless of that, the best way to go is to learn from the past and move forward as quickly as we can.

## ON STARTING AGAIN

Rejuvenation is easier to talk about in books. Getting back to your optimum in reality can be daunting. I have witnessed situations where people give up on their career and simply try to make a living. At different points in our career, we are usually met with the possibility of starting over again, especially when we fail.

What you should know is that the only way to get to your peak is to keep going. Here is one powerful quote that has had amazing impact in my life. This quote popularly attributed to Harriet Tubman goes,

If you are tired, keep going.
If you are scared, keep going.
If you are hungry, keep going.
If you want to taste freedom, keep going.

## BACKUP PLANS

As a matter of fact, plans do not always work just the way we want them to. While we may be able to control many of the strings that influence the success of our plans, those ones we do not have the wherewithal to control can disrupt our plans. The people who build plans that are responsive to change are the ones who withstand disruptions in their plans. When creating a plan, I first look out for the best case scenario. Then I identify all the dependencies that could influence the outcome of the best case scenario. Next, I go through the "what if" exercise around each dependency. For each 'what if' question, I plan for that situation such that when I am done with my plan, I have already considered all the possible scenarios and its effect on that plan.

For example:

Goal

I will get to work tomorrow by 7am so I can prepare the agenda for my meeting.

What are the dependencies?

1. The Company Bus.
2. Wake up time.

What if
1.      What if the company bus does not get here on time?
        Solution: I request for a cab via my ridesharing app.

2.      What if I have no internet?
        Solution: I will get the contact of Sola's cabman and inform him I might need his service.

I used a very simplistic example so it is relatable. Asking the "what ifs" brings more scenarios into view. This way, you can efficiently plan for each scenario to the best of your ability. In the end, what this does is that it confirms to you that you have done your best and left no stones unturned in achieving your desired goals.

## BALANCING WORK AND LIFE

The concept of balancing work with life cannot be overemphasised. If you have been reading this book diligently, I am sure you would have come up with several things you look forward to doing as you start to take action. In the midst of this, it is possible to get lost in the world of work.

One of the things to keep at the back of your mind is that building a conscious career is usually a means to an end. The quality of your life should ultimately improve due to the progress of your career. I do not believe you should lose your life in the quest for a great career. On the other hand, your quest for a great career should ultimately make your life more fulfilling. This way, you continue to value your life, your contributions and the lives of the people around you and their contributions. This includes your family, friends and immediate community.

I agree that there are times when you are unable to attend to family duties because of work. While this is understandable it should never become a habit. You should not see it as normal to neglect your family for work. Neither should you do so for your health and other commitments that affect your quality of life. What you should seek to do instead is create a balance. Find a way to keep your commitments to these two sides of your life. It is possible to have a great career and a great life. You must tell yourself this till it becomes your reality. While building a fulfilling career, make sure you are investing in the people who can share in your success.

## CAREER GROWTH TRACKER

"A journey of a thousand miles begins with one step." - Lao Tzu

A primary method you can use to take the leap is to break it into smaller goals. As I discussed previously, when you make progress in each step you take, you are more likely to take more steps. Your desire to build a successful career is huge and the only way to achieve it is by breaking it down into actionable goals. I call the template below Growth Tracker. You should only input the important goals that will lead to your career growth in this tracker. Remember that creating this template for yourself will mean nothing if you do not commit to executing the actions you outline. I would like you to make a copy of this Growth Tracker for yourself and use it along with the action plan we created in Chapter Eight.

| Areas of Development (What area important to my career do I need to develop?) | Development goals (What is my target for this area?) | Action steps (What do I need to do to reach this goal?) | Milestones (What goals do I need to reach to ensure I am progressing?) | Estimated Completion date (When do I expect to complete these action steps?) | Obstacles (What obstacles can I potentially face trying to reach this goal?) | Solutions (How do I intend to tackle these obstacles?) | Evaluation Criteria (How do I measure my progress and know if I have succeeded?) |
|---|---|---|---|---|---|---|---|
| Public Speaking | Able to deliver a 10 minute speech in front of an audience without stuttering. | - Take public speaking training. - Practice once a week on a popular speech. | - Deliver a speech in front of an audience. - Deliver a speech in front of an audience within the allotted time | 10th September 2018 | Demanding work hours | - Mix offline classes with online sessions. | - Ask my public speaking coach to grade my performance. - Ask audience what they think about and learnt from my performance. |

## GETTING A CAREER ADVISOR

One of the things a lot of people in advanced countries benefit from is the ease with which they can access the services of a career advisor. One of my friends once said that in developed countries, they make it so hard for you to fail. While this might be exaggerated, I do understand her point. In a country where you barely ever get a proper guide to lead you as you make career choices, it is very easy to make the wrong career choices which could have negative effects in the long run. If you fall into the category of people who have never used the guidance of a career advisor or counsellor, which is more common in Nigeria, it is not too late to speak to one. What a career advisor offers is to provide you with a broader view of any field you have chosen. A career advisor also helps you to understand what you need to excel in that field and how you may reach the peak in that field. Some career advisors are very good at matching your talent with a field they feel might be best for you. Other times, they open you up to different fields you may adapt your talent and skills to pursue.

While there are many people who may have attained success without the help of career advisors, consulting one increases your chances as they help you make informed decisions that ultimately affect your career success.

## BUILD TO LAST

The lure of a fulfilling and financially rewarding career can sometimes lead people on different paths. The quest to build a great career can cause you to do unimaginable things. I have been privileged to see how some people who built great careers end. Quite a number ended up unhappy though it appeared as if they reached the peak, while some others became even more successful at the end of their careers. All this is to say, I hope you learn that building a great career is not enough; building a career that deliberately harnesses your passion and expertise for impact should be your ultimate goal.

The first step to greatness in your career journey is your belief that you can do it, and it continues with the actions you commit to taking every day. You are work in progress, just as I am. This is not the end. This is just the beginning of your career success. Be conscious.